THE WAR FIGHTER'S GUIDE

RICHARD CONANT

Copyright © 2002
Richard Conant

All rights reserved. No part of this book may be reproduced in any form, except for the inclusion of brief quotations in a review, without permission in writing from the author or publisher.

ISBN: 0-9725586-0-8

Printed in the United States by:
Morris Publishing
3212 East Highway 30
Kearney, NE 68847
1-800-650-7888

ACKNOWLEDGEMENTS

Whenever I've read a book and came upon the Acknowledgement section, I always thumbed right past it, giving it a smirk and a "Good grief" attitude. But after all the sweating and grunting, and all the physical and mental torment the keyboard gave me, as I was writing this book... an "Ack" to a few people is the least I can do to show my sincere appreciation. "Thanks Honey" to my wife, Blanca. To Pastor Pa^{t}ul Kummer, my human spiritual leader and counselor, "You're definitely More Than a Conqueror!" Martha Lucia, my Ultimate Warrior, and special thanks to Dorothy Wise for speaking my vision and taking me on as a spiritual mentor.

Without each of you, your encouragement, your barbed humor, and your prophetic senses, I would not have been able to blaze this trail. Thanx.

FOREWORD

The Foreword is usually a section within a book comprised of a bunch of words the author wants to say prior to starting with the meat. So it is with this Foreword. I thought it was necessary to put these comments and statements up front to provide the reader with a greater situational awareness (i.e. a mental image) of the operational environment when mere mortals encounter God or one of His representatives.

The Prelude and Introduction of this book form an initial starting block for the reader, prior to jumping directly into the "Combat Zone" of the book. A unique section not seen in other books is the Backword (i.e. usually a section comprised of a bunch of words the author wants to say after finishing with the meat, but still wanting to save a little room for savoring a dessert). This is the antithesis of the Foreword. In the Backword, other disparate ideas related to spiritual combat are addressed; however these do not necessarily lend themselves toward any essential foundational element(s). That's the reason for them being addressed in the Backword.

Additionally, for those not familiar with certain military terminology, there is a Glossary and list of several acronyms complete with definitions and explanations offered in the Appendix. Yes, the Appendix is in back of the Backword.

Many people are not aware that the same skills and principles taught to become efficient and effective, earthly warfighters are actually based on biblical precedence and teachings. This guide brings to light several of these areas by going back to the source, the Bible. These will greatly assist the earthly and spiritual warfighter in surviving, *eternally.*

You've certainly heard the saying, "*War is hell.*" Based on this, I submit to you:

"[Without spiritual] *War*[fare, there] *is* [certainly] *hell* [awaiting]."

CONTENTS

Prelude

Introduction

Preparation

1. Training
2. Basic Training
3. TEAM Principles
4. TEAM Requirements
5. Synchro-Congruency
6. TEAM Operations
7. Responsibility
8. Discipline
9. Vigilance
10. Discipleship
11. Advanced Training
12. Specialty Skills
13. Testing
14. Trials
15. Suffering
16. Technical School
17. Learning & Understanding

18. Intelligent Preparation for the Battlefield (IPB)

The Armory

19. "Armor!!!"
20. Sword of the Spirit
21. Shield of Faith
22. Helmet of Salvation
23. Breastplate of Righteousness
24. Belt of Truth
25. Shoes of the Gospel of Peace

Battle Management

26. BMC4
27. Centralized Command - Decentralized Execution
28. Rules Of Engagement
29. Command by Negation
30. Special Instructions
31. Joint Multi-Tactical Digital Information Link Operating Procedures
32. Interoperability
33. Joint and Coalition Forces
34. Integration – The Key
35. Ode to the Warfighter

Combat Missions

36. Combat Search and Rescue
37. Psychological Operations
38. Sabotage/Espionage
39. Servicing the Target

Courses of Action

40. Action
41. Amen
42. OutBrief
43. Backword

Appendix A: Glossary and Acronyms

PRELUDE

If the original Biblical authors had the technological backing that authors have today, I'm betting the Bible would have been written a little bit differently. Their writings, letters, and psalms would be filled with emotionally charged, bolded large font and exclamation points followed by bullet-spitting declaratives. These would depict actual activities occurring throughout the Bible. However, these representative writings would have pushed the production of the scrolls and Bible, as we know them today, way to the right. In essence, it would have made the publishing available at a much later date. Furthermore, scientific calculations estimate that it would have required 36.59 times more ink, papyrus, styluses, and miscellaneous supplies.

Who says we don't have a benevolent God? He certainly knew the confusion it would have wreaked, if He requested a true [fontal] representation of even just the more significant events recorded. Nevertheless, think how much more life-like reading the Bible would be if it were written with today's technology to depict the true emotional attributes of the author or described participant. Let's consider just the following passage with Moses. I'll attempt to more fully depict the situation as it probably really occurred.

Put yourself in the shoes, and mental framework of Moses during his encounter with the burning bush, OK? You're a shepherd, out in the grassy countryside with your sheep. You're not thinking about anything scientifically stimulating or

waiting for the Beach Boys to sing "Endless Summer". The only thing you have on your mind is:
- the weather
- picking out certain sheep for slaughter
- keeping a vigilant eye out for sheep rustlers and wild nefarious animals
- watching your step so you don't mess up your sandals.

Got it? All right. That's the mental state we are, and Moses, was in. Then,

> Exodus 3:2b *"Moses saw the bush afire and that it wasn't burning up."*

Now you tell me what would be going through your shepherd's head given this data dump on mixing fire with dry bush tinder. Let's step back one. In the days of Moses, fire was a highly desired commodity. Afterall, during this period, Zippo wasn't available. Fire was still made by spinning sticks and clicking rocks together.

Moses was sharp. He knew something unusual was going on. Not only because there was this bush out in the middle of nowhere burning, all by itself; but furthermore, the fire wasn't consuming the bush. It was just blazing away, pillaring with flames and smoke. Take a minute to absorb this and put yourself in the proper mental state to deal with this phenomenon and then read on.

> Exodus 3:3 *"So Moses said, I will step aside right now and examine this wonderful sight, why the thornbush is not burned up."*

This all sounds so matter of fact, doesn't it? It almost sounds like a precursor speech to something that Shakespeare would come up with. That's because, in that time, they didn't have expressions like "Whoa! Back the truck up, dude!" "Whassup with this?"

When Moses saw the bush blazing away, he didn't ponder this sight, stroke his beard and think, "Oh what an abnormally peculiar phenomenon this portrays to my receptor sensors." On the contrary, his head and whole body snapped around after the double take. Kinda like the Tasmanian Devil, when Taz's head pops out of the tornado.

I'll tell you with all confidence, Moses is now entering the initial phases of shock trauma syndrome. You know how it is when you get in an accident and everything all of a sudden switches to slow motion? This is the state Moses is in. His heart rate is going about 200 beats per minute, but his mind is in a "cool down zone" trying to protect the body from entering a certain state of shock. OK. Check your pulse.

You still with me? Let's continue.

> Exodus 3:4a *"The Lord saw him turn aside to observe and God called to him from the bush: Moses, Moses!"*

We know God has a naturally commanding voice. Many of you have experienced heat lightning on a humid night in the Southeast, or finger lightning spreading through the skies in Tucson, AZ, followed by the heavy tympani of ro-o-l-l-ling thunder. God's voice is like that, a clean mix of sky-rippling lightning and hurricane-tearing thunder. This is especially accurate when His speaking is actually annotated with exclamation marks in the Bible. You can be most certain when God speaks in an exclamatory manner that the mountains are shaking, their rocks are sliding down into the valleys, the nearby stream is bubbling fiercely, and the fish in it are starting to float upside down. All just from the sound of His voice.

Now, let's regroup on this verse. The Lord didn't say, "Moses, Moses." like one of those soft, sexy answering machine voices. In His voice of thunder and lightning clashing, God said, "**Moses! Moses!!!**" Envision the reaction. Put yourself in Moses' sandals and mental state, again. Here's an actual recovered clip taken from Moses' brain:

> "Whoa, baby! Moses, this is your brain speaking. That burning bush just shouted out your name. I can't keep the body under control. Circuit breakers are popping. Warning lights are flashing. Alarms are clanging! Moses, are you there buddy…?"

Have you ever played the game where you run out to a baseball bat, put one end on the ground and your head on the other end, and then run five circles around it? When you try to run back to the starting point, things get a little woozy, right? Well, Moses' body and brain are in a major "woozy" right about now. He must have made some kind of [probable near-comatose] remark because the Bible goes on to say:

> Exodus 3:4b "*God answered. Here I am. [5] Then He said, Do not move nearer! Take your sandals off your feet, for the place on which you are standing is holy ground.*"

I think God probably said this, intending to benefit us (todays warfighters) because God knew Moses' body wasn't going anywhere under these current circumstances. Moses was probably trying to get his body and brain to repulse the internal and external ongoing convulsions. If Moses could have replied, it probably would have been with a statement along these lines:

> "Oh, most merciful Lord. Have no doubts. I certainly can't move, let alone any closer. My face is now in the dirt because my legs are jello; my backbone has turned to water and I need to change my underwear. Have no doubts, O mighty force from God, I'll not be moving any time soon!"

After Moses' encounter with God, I can understand the apprehension Moses must have felt prior to coming back to the Israeli camp. Put yourself back in his sandals. What would be the belief factor, if you were out wandering around in the mountains and came back from your hike with news that you had seen a non-burning, flaming bush and, God spoke to you. How do you think people would respond to you? Would they offer to put a cool cloth across your forehead? Or request you sit down, put your feet up for a while and offer you something to drink?

Aside from the direct observation that Moses now probably wore a sportingly deep suntan from the UV/radiation exposure and "wired" hair from talking with God: Do you think this would get people to fall in line behind Moses and follow him without question? Putting all these different variables into an equation is something similar to analyzing the Greek symbology for differential calculus after just learning in elementary school math that you can now use a " • " instead of an "**x**" for multiplying.

Does that make it a little bit clearer? These guys, that God honored, mentioned in the Bible are just like you and me. They have feelings. They pump adrenoline when excited, and suffer frustration when things aren't going as expected. Check it out. Don't get in the trap that all these guys were stoic, unemotional, Dudly-Do-Right flatliners.

Therefore, when you read this guide, and the Bible, put yourself in the actual environment. As you would envision it happening today. Make it a literal occurrence in your life.

INTRODUCTION

Welcome to The Warfighters Guide to successfully engaging the enemy in spiritual combat. This work depicts a delicate representation for those who are chosen to travel down the wooded trails, bike paths, and highways of spiritual warfare. I've painstakingly directed the warfighter to enjoy the pleasures along the roadside, to take in all the aspects of nature: the smell of the blooming flowers, the sound of the birds chirping, and the drone from the buzzing bees.

What? Who am I trying to kid? Let's cut the crap and get with it. This book is about combat. Spiritual Warfare. Prepare to hear the clanking of heavy armor, the sight of heavily burdened warfighters lugging backpacks and gear: tired, weary, wounded bodies shuffling toward the objective.

Spiritual warfare is an intense and dangerous activity. It is a specific task, a mission especially assigned by Jesus to His selected. Not everyone is chosen to serve and function in this environment. Therefore this guide is prepared for those:

- Who feel they are appointed to go toe-to-toe with Satan
- Who want to be known as the enemy of Satan
- Who want to invoke the Lord's prayer: *"God's will be done, on earth as it is in heaven."*

This book, unlike the current political climate wherein administrators and bureaucrats are trying to turn swords into plowshares, ...this book is intended for those who are chosen or who have a desire to turn their spiritual plowshares into sharpened swords for Jesus. This book is for spiritual warfighters: snake eaters, shooters, and SEABEES (Nehemiah 4:17,18).

In a hostile environment, before the soil can be plowed, tilled, fertilized and seeds planted, the "land" must first be conquered. Warfighters are needed to engage the enemy, secure the perimeter, and be on guard! To Watch! These actions are absolutely mandatory. After the snake eaters and shooters establish themselves, the SEABEES, with their heavy construction equipment, are the next warriors to come in and establish a presence. They scratch the ground clean, lay the foundation to build airstrips and operational facilities for the Commander and forward deployed forces. The SEABEES serve as a transitory force from the special ops guys to the combat logisticians and administrative teams because they are still armed. They are multi-tasked in not only clearing the land, but also for keeping Watch! Yes, that is why they carry weapons while turning a hostile environment into a pliable workable arena, amenable for the conduct of combat operations. This is the function of the spiritual warfighter: to successfully engage Satan and his forces; to secure the perimeter against enemy forays and intrusions; to lay a solid foundation and the required structures for a growing Task Force in the name of Jesus, our Commander.

For those so chosen, read on. (Note: If you're just curious, or if your desire is high for becoming a warfighter, you may also still continue reading. But be cognizant that some of my statements may make the curious feel intimidated. This may occur because my focus is specifically directed toward the warfighter.) The inherent functions and requirements for combat operations are completely different than those requirements for a pastoring, a caring, or a service ministry. Warfighters using this guide as a Concept of Operations (CONOP) will certainly enhance their warfighting skills and increase their ratio for successfully engaging the enemy. However, all must take heed of the following:

WARNING:

Those who walk up front and out in the open are susceptible to being continuously fired upon.

Don't accept this task unless God has put you in these combat boots, specifically. For those of you still directed to take this course of action:

Hooah! Hoo-YAH! Hallelu-JAH! AMEN!

In your pursuit of receiving the title of Warfighter, remember:
*God has NOT given us a spirit of fear, but rather a spirit of **POWER** and **SELF-DISCIPLINE*** (2Tim 1:7).

He encouragingly yells at us:

***BE STRONG! BE COURAGEOUS!** Do **NOT** be terrified. **Do NOT** be discouraged. I, the*

Lord your God will be with you wherever you go! Joshua 1:9.

We've already described the qualities of God's voice. He does not speak in a *mamsy-pamsy* manner. Look again. He said, "I will be with you <u>wherever</u> you go." That means he'll also be with you wherever and whenever you stop: to rest, to regroup, and to reconnoiter.

After putting this CONOP into practice,
Don't be surprised when Jesus looks down, and
Points His finger toward you, and
Declares to His angels and all the heavenlies:

"Now that dog can hunt!"

"Blessed be the Lord my strength, which teaches my hands to wage war, and my fingers to do battle;" Psalms 144:1

Preparation

Chapter One—

Training

Transforming a person into an earthly, effective warfighter requires more than just putting on combat boots and BDUs (Battle Dress Uniform). It takes training. Training to learn new skills. Training to brush up on old skills, and training to modify the old skills to fit into new environments. Proper training is a time zone. It takes months and sometimes years of direction, guidance and focus to acquire and become proficient in specialized skills. A warfighter never really "graduates" from training because new skills applicable to new circumstances are always needed. Training is a process that continually hones the physical and mental capabilities; that prepares the warfighter for combat operations; that turns the combatant into an effective warfighter.

Training for battle ensures the immediate execution of critical tasks during combat. In combat there always isn't time to look up an Operations Order, flip the pages of a checklist to configure equipment, or refer to an electrical schematic to troubleshoot a malfunctioning panel prior to weapons release. These things need to be known! Any delay in action can be deadly.

Furthermore, transformation into an effective warfighter truly begins when an individual realizes it takes a team effort to learn, understand, and apply the theoretical principles of warfighting. This is exactly the same in spiritual warfare. It takes a functional application of putting our eyes on Jesus (focus, continuous prayer) and executing our faith [stepping out and activating His gifts] with our whole heart in order to continue to receive His direction. Becoming an effective, spiritual warfighter is more than just silently acknowledging, "Jesus is Lord [mumble, mumble...]," it is an emphatic mental decision process! Like any other skill builder, it requires definite action to complete the transition to accomplishment. Only through action can the mission (His personal tasking for you) be successfully executed! Rest assured that this "Action" element is discussed thoroughly throughout this book.

One other topic I need to ensure is properly addressed is, Maturity. Spiritual Maturity. As in combat, the seasoned combat veterans have not only finished their training courses, but they've put the theories and principles to work in an operational environment. Combat veterans come in all ranks, from Private to Colonel. They also come in all ages, from teenager to gray [or no] haired adult. A combat veteran is determined by operational experience, not by age, rank, title, or position. Similarly, in spiritual combat, experience is the determining factor.

Gran'ma said, "Either you is, or you isn't." There's no in between. Age, rank, name, title, genetic heritage, etc. have absolutely no bearing on combat experience. These elements are not discriminators in quantitatively assessing the degree of combat experience of a warfighter. A teenager, and even pre-teens, can have the anointed power and authority generally assumed for a 30+ year practicing pastor.

Training does not discriminate. It's purpose is to raise the bar regarding our abilities. It ensures we all, yes ALL of us, rely on the same foundational principles and procedures. Training further enhances the warfighter's confidence, timing, and sense of urgency. Are you ready? Ok, let's get going!

Chapter Two—

Basic Training

Basic Training provides the warfighter with the first step toward receiving proper training. Basic Training is the "playing field" for us to learn, to inject new techniques into our databases, and then to incorporate and apply these techniques, i.e. team building, and elements into our warfighting lifestyle.

Many people will automatically reject the notion that their lifestyle is currently operating in a war, a combat engagement zone. They will indeed reject the notion that they are already a participant in an ongoing, unseen war. They have become accustomed to this status and accept it as the norm. This "notional existence" is rationalized by the scientific, experiential portion of our minds.

It's fairly similar to the first time you walked on a trampoline or were assigned to ship-duty. You experienced an uncertainty whenever you stepped because of the flex in the trampoline's surface or the roll of the sea; but after a while you became used to it. As a matter of fact, you didn't realize how fast you became acclimated until you actually jumped off the trampoline and hit the ground (BIG surprise), or when you walked back on-shore and your "land legs" haven't yet engaged.

And so it is with many of us today. We have become accustomed to the sound of artillery rounds zooming by, mortar shells exploding in our proximity, and automatic weapons being fired at us.

We take this for daily activity. Things that we alone have to contend with. Things that we have absolutely no control over.

Wait a second... isn't that a cop-out? Isn't that like calling ourselves prepared for a hostile encounter when in all actuality we're acting just like Barney Fife? We've got our gun, oiled and strapped down in its holster. We've got our bullet in our shirt pocket. Buttoned down, of course. Just waiting for Andy to give us permission to put it in the chamber.

Let's quit kidding ourselves, Ok? If we're going to be real warfighters, not wannabees, then we're going to have to not only talk the talk, but walk the walk. We're going to have to live the life of a warfighter, learn the appropriate tactics, techniques, and procedures and be committed to this "new" lifestyle.

This is what Basic Training is all about. It is the initial foray into realizing what it's going to take for the person willing [or tasked] to become a warfighter. It is the entry point toward beginning/accepting the lifestyle of a warfighter.

Yes, it is going to be necessary to study warfighting doctrine, concepts of operations, standard operating procedures, etc. No, it is not required to be swamped by all the military manuals, pamphlets, regulations, and joint papers published on these topics. That's the beauty of this one guide. Most people are not aware that the same skills and principles taught to become efficient and effective, earthly warfighters are actually based on biblical precedence and teachings. This guide brings to light several of these areas by going back to the source, the Bible. These will greatly assist the earthly and spiritual warfighter in conquering the enemy. These will assist the ultimate warrior in conquering the enemy and surviving, *eternally*.

The purpose of Basic Training is to give the warfighter, His information to train properly. To be properly equipped, to use the tools and weapons intended. To let the warfighter hunt and eat meat. To let him war effectively with His weapons, for His purpose.

Chapter Three—

TEAM Principles

In this section, we'll be addressing several key team elements: mental preparation, physical training, synchro-congruency, SOS [not the food], interdependence, responsibility, and discipline. These team elements are not the end-all, do-all comprehensive elements to ensure a driven, smart warrior. Rather they form the foundation [i.e. start the process] for a successful warfighter and warfighting team.

Up to this point many of us have been out in the world, doing the best we can, working hard for what we want to acquire and accomplish as an individual. Most have been fighting their own personal battles. Some have taken on a Rambo mentality ("I'll do it my way no matter what!") to realize their objectives. While others are satisfied with their accomplishments based on more personable attributes than Rambo. However, probably all query the real need for being a member of a team.

Most of us have played team sports during our school years and recognize the benefits of playing on a well-organized team. It's a simplistic fact to acknowledge that a single individual cannot win, for example, a football game against an opposing team. We recognize basic team elements every Monday night during football season. It's quite obvious when the players aren't playing as a team. Why is it then that we haven't taken these obviously apparent benefits and implemented them into our own personal and spiritual lives? Why is it that we only use these team principles on the playing field, when we're with our friends and want to leave the workweek behind? We know team elements can provide great benefit toward reaching goals. We know they work, but we don't seriously integrate them into our daily lives. Even more importantly, we don't use them when we especially need them in our spiritual lives, when we conduct combat operations. Why?

The main reason is: We are hung up on being a solo hunter, providing for one's self and family. We're responsible to others. We don't have time to do something different. Team stuff is for the playing field. It takes too much time to train, to work with others, to overcome obstacles and interface with everyone else, blah, blah, blah. If any of these excuses is your "reason," let me give you a harsh Wake-Up call:

Everything in God's kingdom is based on the Team. God matures, makes, and then uses His skilled workers to accomplish His purposes. He activates concentrated teams to lead His assigned efforts. His skilled craftsmen and leaders are required to ensure His will is executed accurately accordingly to His plan. No lone rangers are allowed. Everyone must be accountable and under the authority of someone else. [Hey, even the Lone Ranger wasn't alone. Remember Tonto?]

In the physical [sports] world, this person is known as the Coach. He counsels, trains, plans and strategizes for the team, based on the strengths of each member and on the team as a whole. In the spiritual realm, this person is acknowledged as the pastor, prophet, or apostle.

They counsel, train, plan and strategize the offensive prior to actual combat engagement for the spiritual warfighter. Think about it. This team interaction actually reduces the risk for each combatant. Mull that one over.

You've got two immediate options. Right now:

1. Close the book and put it back on the shelf; or
2. Buckle your seat belt and keep reading to find out what Jesus wants us to do.

For the benefit of those who are still reading and for those who were more involved with one-on-one sports and interaction (e.g. boxing, racquetball, checkers, or Mario), and even for those who weren't actively exposed to a working team environment, let's get some Situational Awareness (SA) on the word "team." This will enable everyone to operate from the same sheet of music. OK? The word "Team" is actually an acronym meaning:

Together
Everyone
Achieves
More

Intrinsic to the noun, Team, is its verbness. The letter "A" in TEAM stands for Achieves. Achieves, is a present tense verb. In order for an achievement to occur, action is required. Yes! You got it. A Team ACTs! That's what it is meant to do. If it isn't doing; if it isn't filled with Do-ers, it becomes bored and subsequently turns into a board, or a committee. No, that is not a play on words. Too many of the Commander's orders and tasks have ended up in a committee where they were literally "talked to [their] death."

This is a favorite tactic of many Action Offices. [What an abhorrent title to assume!] Filled with non-decision makers, they decide, not to decide and thereafter alter, impede, and lay the foundations of failure for the Commander's objectives. It's adamant we don't get caught in these man-made traps that can thwart even the best efforts by a warfighter.

Now, back to the acronym. A brilliant, working example of real teamwork follows. No, I'm not slapping myself on the back for coming up with this one. The literal "brilliance" will be self-evident after reading the analogy below.

We've all used a candle to provide light. Gazing upon the candle's light is often a quieting experience. For it yields a beautiful peaceful light, but at times frustratingly weak. For one candle by itself is weak. Its flame is susceptible to being snuffed out by any change in activity, wind, or breeze. Thereby providing only a glimmer, or a flickering and fluttering light. Not strong enough to complete a task effectively or efficiently.

As individuals we are like a candle (one single candle = one candlepower) only providing its own light. A weak light, but nevertheless a light, provided by Jesus. This light is a beginning, a first step toward attaining a true Light for Jesus.

Many candles (e.g. 100 candles = 100 candlepower) together magnify the Light. Hey, a beacon is now forming. Fanning the flame (i.e. Action! Activity! Combat!) magnifies the candlepower by orders of magnitude. This is the start of founding a Lighthouse.

When one person is joined by others, a team is formed. A working TEAM is capable of being that Lighthouse for others.

Make us a Lighthouse Lord! A beacon in the night. A solid, firm foundation that beams a steady, guaranteed light and provides direction even in the worst raging storm. Count on us Lord to be strong. To be leaders of the weak. To rescue those that are in danger. Count on us to be there in times of turmoil. Storm-tossed nights. Count on us to shine through the evil darkness of Satan. To expose the Truth, the Light that You are. Let us be counted as ones that are steadfast and true to the course.

Shoot. Let's significantly increase the age-old Lighthouse with a little technology. Ok? We now have the wherewithal and knowledge of how to become a beacon for others... how about polishing up some mirrors and aiming them into a single focal point. What's that? A laser beam! Let's employ our concentrated efforts (i.e. a laser) to knock out, confuse, disorient, and destroy any weapons employed by the Opposition Force (OPFOR). Just like a laser beam is used to confuse, disorient or destroy the electronics in a weapon, a well-trained, action-oriented team can confuse, disorient, and destroy the enemy by tipping it off balance. This is accomplished when the team displays synchronized unpredictability, daring, and surprise. Even a cluster of individuals (lighthouses) cannot accomplish this. It takes extraordinary focus (lasers) from the team. [We'll talk about these elements in further detail in a later section (PsyOps/CCD).] Let's take the Strategic Defense Initiative (SDI) and use it for a Strategic Offensive Initiative (SOI). Lord, help us to take the fight to Satan. Help us to become a Spiritual

Offensive Initiative. Make us a Laser beam Lord! Semper Fi. Amen!

The warfighter must acknowledge another important element: The enemy exists as a team, a professionally experienced, fierce, opposition force. Back the truck up. The opposing team? You mean there really is a spiritual OPFOR and it is [already] organizationally structured and operating as a team in our present physical world?

Yes, the opposition does exist. As a matter of fact, the OPFOR Commander is a rogue Colonel known by the names Satan, Lucifer, and the Devil. The OPFOR has been in existence for at least a couple thousand years. It's composed of highly experienced, well-trained, and enthusiastic forces. And yes, they are organized. The OPFOR can run highly synchronized covert operations, guerrilla ops, and even bold, all out frontal assaults simultaneously. Manpower, money, and time do not restrict them. O&M (Operations and Management) and RDT&E (Research, Development, Testing and Evaluation) funding is always brimming full. Assets are never in short supply. Currently, the OPFOR is impervious to defeat, setbacks, and embarrassment. They relentlessly persist in trying to weaken their foe, i.e. Jesus' warfighters.

Let that sink in for a bit.

OK. Ready to continue?

We all know the outcome of one person playing football, baseball, hockey, etc. against a well organized, disciplined, professional team. We all recognize how ridiculous that person would be to think, or even consider, that he could score against the opposing team. How much more ridiculous is it to even attempt to engage the spiritual OPFOR in combat as a single individual? Realize also, the stakes are much higher than playing a game of football with your buds, or making a bet. These stakes have a lasting, eternal impact.

Now, are there any questions regarding why we need to be absolutely dedicated? To operate more effectively and more efficiently than we have been?

Check out what God said regarding combat effectiveness!

> Heb12:1b *let us get rid of every impediment*

This includes the excuses and the blah, blah, blah "reasons" to attempt to tough it out by ourselves.

> *and the sin that ensnares us so easily,*

As a single soldier, we're not maximizing the potential of our brain and body. We're susceptible to ambushes and booby-traps. Even small wounds and obstacles will take a toll on our body and effort. We just can't make good combat-effective progress with only one set of eyes.

> *and let us run steadily the course mapped out for us*

This is what Basic Training is all about. This is the first step in becoming a spiritual warfighter. Shed the myopia associated with "I." Let loose of our own personal desires and procedures for accomplishing actions. We were meant to be on a warfighting team. We engage the enemy as one whole. We enable the strongest to lead. Look at the Common Tactical Picture (CTP), the big picture. Our goal is to win the war, and accomplish the objectives Jesus has assigned to us.

[2a] with our eyes on Jesus,
Focus. Focus! Focus!! How many times did your coach or Drill Instructor shout that? Don't let your eyes wander. Don't be distracted. Keep the notch in your sights filled. Keep the cross-hairs on the target. Focus on what's important. Keep your eyes on the goal. Even more important than your own personal rampaging, hysteric D.I., this is God, in your face, telling you what to do. How can you choose not to listen?

Chapter Four—

TEAM Requirements

Prior to a team actually forming to conduct combat operations, the individual team members themselves must first learn certain fundamental skills and pre-designated tasks. Two immediate requirements that individual warfighters must satisfy are:
1. Mental Preparation and
2. Physical Training.

As an individual, one's mental processor either receives (input) or disseminates (output) information (that's called: half duplex) through one serial port. It's a solo operation. A representative model of this is playing a game of marbles by yourself: consideration of other players and coordination of effort is not required. You can win, lose, and draw, as well as none of the above, and the outcome is still the same.

However, as a member of a team, one's mental processor requires at least one parallel port. Input and output is full duplex. Information (mega-data) is flowing in and out simultaneously from numerous input and output sources, i.e. multiple pathways. To properly process and act on these information streams, a great deal of mental preparation is required. These new mental processing techniques and capabilities don't occur in a warfighter without pain, practice, and training. They require a change in the mental processing, perception, and priorities list.

Physical training is part and parcel to this package. (Forgive me, but my Gran'ma always said "part & parcel" to emphasize important elements in an overall concept. Such as, kernel corn and catchin' Tennessee mud trout.... part & parcel.) We need to stress the physical training element as an emphatic, integrated part of mental preparation. In order to attain and keep a high degree of mental dexterity during combat, a physically healthy body is a must. The coach's maxim of "a healthy body yields a healthy mind" not only has a lot of merit, but it is also definitely true.

If you really believe (1Cor 6:19) that your body is literally the temple of the Holy Spirit inside, then we need to consider and monitor what kind of sacrificial food we place on the altar inside as an offering. How healthy is the Holy Spirit, as well as our own body, when the main [sacrificial?] offerings are:

Hot BBQ'd deep fried pork rinds
Southern fried chicken
Biscuits and sausage gravy
[Floating in] diet coke or light beer
Health food: raisins and nuts--- chocolate covered of course, and
Key lime pie

I know this might be stretching it a bit, unless you live in Lower Alabama. However, I'm trying to make a point: We really need to consider what food we bring into the temple for our offerings. Really.

Things have certainly changed since the days in the Old Testament, when the people had to literally present the best of their harvest to the temple, but the principles still remain the same. Our temple is the first encounter others have of Jesus who lives inside of us. First impressions occur with the initial "first" look at the physical structure. Any structure or entity, whether it is a car, a sword, another person, or a church undergoes this same "first" look. We are the physical representation of the Holy Spirit. Although it may not be feasible to work out in the gym all day long, to eat only naturally healthy foods, or to wear three pounds of makeup in order to make our bodies generically appealing (?), we need to be cognizant of what we place on our internal altar.

We also need to consider what pieces of furniture are put in our temple. What types of furniture and materials are not appropriate for a temple? These are questions each of us needs to ask ourselves. We need to consider the answer in accordance with God's direction for us, and then lay our foundation, build the walls, raise the roof and make the Holy Spirit comfortable.

Again, it's of great importance to ensure the Holy Spirit resides in an environment fit for His work. The outer physical structure does need to represent Jesus. Most importantly, however, the outer structure within, needs to have a beacon, a laser that shines with His light. I guess I've been beating around the bushes and running around the same concentric short track. What I'm really trying to get across to you is:

Do your eyes, face, and smile flash the Light of the Holy Spirit?

Is there an aura about you that physically screams out to passersby that:

"I am a friend of Jesus!"

"I provide harbor for the Holy Spirit in my soul."

Get it?
Got it!
Good!

Chapter Five—

Synchro-Congruency

Let's continue to drill it in: Vigorous preparation, practice, and training are needed to effectively become a team. Looking, listening and acting on the guidance and direction of those who have authority over us (coach, pastor, prophet, apostle, etc.) enables us to overcome the "solo" deliberation we naturally lean toward. This, thereby enables us to progress into the advanced realm of "team operations." Recognizing and using the benefits inherent in a [true] team composition is mandatory for effectively engaging, defeating and overcoming the enemy.

A well-trained "synchro-congruent" team can overcome a much greater force. What? Synchro-congruent? Where did that come from?

Ok, I coined that term to illustrate the complex convergence of multiple, multi-axis information sources and paths simultaneously fighting for recognition within the warfighter's mental processor.

Whew!

Hey, I warned you about this, back in the beginning of this section.

Take a breath.

Ready for more?

Let's look closer at what synchro-congruent could possibly mean. We won't do a detailed DNA chain tracing. Rather, let's just take synchro-congruent apart to display it's relatively simple meaning and illustrate its huge impact.

Synchro: Derives from its root word, synchronize.

Synchronize: an action word meaning to orchestrate; to coordinate many activities into a single, smooth flow. Think of a song writer/composer writing a piece of music for a large philharmonic orchestra. Each note blending, yet differentiating itself individually into a smooth flowing, musical motion.

Congruent: another action word meaning to fit harmoniously; a match of power, strength and intellect. Let's use football as an action oriented example.

> The Front Four linemen hunker down and await the snap of the ball. Their mission is to blow a hole in the OPFOR nanoseconds before the Running Back harmoniously wedges his body through the [temporarily] matching gap in the line to grab some badly needed yardage.

Can you see the synchro-congruent team exuding power, strength, intellect, timing, and flow? All the operatives are in motion, simultaneously. Each independent action moving separately, yet in sync and congruent with other forces to accomplish a pre-designated mission.

In today's sports oriented culture, these principles are readily identifiable. One person or a cluster of individuals can't effectively compete against a team. Therefore, a working "arrangement" with the other individuals is absolutely necessary to establish an effective, working team. This "arrangement" must first denote or list each individual's specific duty and function along with their required performance objectives. For the benefit of data geeks, these objectives are alternatively called Measures of Effectiveness and Measures of Performance (MOEs/MOPs). For the benefit of normal people, allow me to use another example to simplistically illustrate the functionality involved here.

Each person, in the cluster, is assigned a separate position and unique requisite duties. For instance, one person is designated to be the ball-handler. In football that person is called the Quarterback. Here's a simple conversation of the quarterback establishing MOEs and MOPs for the team:

Quarterback: "Everybody, except Bobby Joe, block. I'm throwing the ball to Bobby Joe. Bobby Joe, you blitz down the left for ten yards, do a button hook, and the ball'll be in your chest. Hang on to it and run like a scalded dog."

Although this descriptive doesn't reveal in any specificity the minute details and action objectives (MOEs/MOPs) required for a synchro-congruent team performance, the fundamentals addressed in the first paragraph are easily visualized. Make sense?

Chapter Six—

TEAM Operations

Let's cover two other required fundamental principles that serve as an entry point into establishing an effectively working combat team.
1. Subordination of Self (SOS) and
2. Interdependence on others.

These two "working" elements are among the minimum basic requirements to have a viable effective team, a team capable of effectively combating the OPFOR. The first element, Subordination of Self, doesn't mean to put your own capabilities down. No one wants you to go moping around thinking demeaning, incoherent [stupid] thoughts about yourself or about your capabilities as an individual. Rather, subordination involves a fundamental change in one's priority assessment and perception of importance. It requires a change of focus from "I, me, and my" to "we, ours, and us". It means to yield, to capitulate, to submit, and to present oneself completely without any strings attached. No caveats. No side bets. No money-back guarantees, etc. to the team.
Subordination of Self requires finding out what the goals and objectives are for the team, and then making those goals and objectives your own target. Your previous personal goals and objectives will probably require alterations, modifications or re-prioritization. Getting me, my, and I into the

racing "pole position" will more than likely fall out as not being all that important anymore.

As part of a spiritual warfighting combat team, subordination of your personal desires and self means to willingly endorse yourself as a full-fledged member of the team/fighting corps. Subordination is not only required, but in fact, it is a direct command from the Commander in Chief (CINC) to *Submit yourself to God.* [James 4:7]. Complete submission to God's team is required.

Subordinate your individual wants, wishes, and objectives to those He brings to you. Show Him your willingness to be a warfighter on His team. Do this and He'll provide you with more power, wisdom, and understanding to execute His plan than you could ever have mastered by yourself.

In spiritual combat, we also need to be independently dependable to, and interdependent on the One team leader, Jesus, to enable Him to maximize our journey through this earth-bound, combat-oriented life. This is also a two way street. When we

Draw close(r) *to God, He'll come close*(r) *to us.* [James 4:8].

[Trivia Archival Data Bit:
Q: Who was the original author of the lyrics that you might remember from the song: "Darlin' if you want me to be closer to you, get closer to me."
A: See above.]

The second element, interdependence on others, is a real mouthful, isn't it? Anytime I run into a profusely, inordinate amount of syllables in one word I've gotta back the truck up and decipher what the word is really trying to say. I'm no Yankee doctor, so I've got to have a lot of spaces between my words. Otherwise I get sick and have to go back to Lower Alabama to get a prescription (one that I can read) to get better. Does that make sense? OK. So let's perform a little differential analysis of terminology to depict the functional importance and practical application of "interdependence". (Ouch. There's that trace of Yankee bloodline rising up, again.) Let's break interdependence up into words and terms we readily recognize and understand.

"Depend" implies an environment of reliability, loyalty, steadfastness, a constant condition. In combat operations, depend means one can heavily lean on a designated entity (a person, weapon, or spirit) for support in getting an action or mission accomplished.

For example, harking back to Bobby Joe, "I depend on you to hit me in the chest with that football, so I can score." It's a two way street, man. If the football is off target and I have to jump for it, that extra effort and unplanned action will have a negative performance impact on the desired end result. Several different things could happen. For instance, the OPFOR that's shadowing me could take me out while I'm airborne; my jump might not be well timed or too weak, causing me to miss the ball. Or worse yet, in trying to catch it, I could accidentally tip it into play to the OPFOR.

We've all got to do our individual parts, ... together. As best we can. If one of us doesn't perform at the expected level, the original tasking canNOT be executed as planned. Does that make sense? Does that make the definition of "depend" clearer? Depend is at the root [hence root word, for you grammar geeks] of the word, team. Depend is not a solo action, it involves two or more players and multiple activities.

"Dependent" changes the operational environment a little more. Unlike "depend" where there is pretty much a 50/50 split between participants, "dependent" swings the pendulum to something closer to a 63/37 split. Our personal responsibility still mandates an accountability for our actions. But some of the action's control is placed outside of our own personal hands and entrusted into the hands of other(s).

For instance, Coach calls the play, but the ball must first go from the Center to the Quarterback, before the play takes form. The play is literally out of the coach's hands. But, who is responsible for the performance? Who is the dependent participant? …. Did you have to read that sentence twice? What did you come up with? ALL the players AND the coach are responsible, and yet dependent, also.

Whassup with this, dude? You got it. The pendulum swings. It's still a two-way street. No *Einbahnstraße* here! However, the 63/37 split changes depending on the operational environment. The team players are dependent on the coach to train, teach, and guide them during practice. The coach is dependent on the team players for executing the assigned mission while they are on the [battle] field. The team players are dependent on the coach to refine their performance, issue further guidance and orders for combating the OPFOR, etc. Back and forth. Back and forth. The pendulum keeps swinging from one [dependent] side to the other.

This is the exact representation of how Jesus has directed us as warfighters to operate in the combat zone. This was His original vision. The

way the fight is supposed to be fought. The apostles and prophets lay the groundwork for the battle. The warriors wage the war based on this guidance. The apostles and prophets observe, listen, and issue further guidance and orders, etc. Back and forth. Back and forth. Continuously treading toward the goal.
    Get it?
    Got it!
    OK, let's move on.

    Inter means to put in the ground, to bury. We're not burying our "depend" in the dirt to forget about it. Au contraire, (that's the Cajun in me) we're putting "depend" in the ground surrounded by high-strength concrete, reinforced with steel. This is the foundation. Think of "inter" as in interwoven. Threads finely intertwined yielding strength measured in leaps of magnitude beyond the single strand. Not yielding to breakage. Each individual thread performing its bonding function to ultimately achieve the strength of a steel cable. Each thread is part and parcel to the whole body, unique in composition, yet indistinguishable from the whole. It provides a shield to the innermost body. Yet even the innermost body, the core, is intergrated (give me a break on the spelling, I'm trying to make a point here, OK?) as one consummate part, a team.
    That's what interdependent means. It interweaves the subordination of individual capabilities and independence, into a meshing of an interactive, interdependent, synergistic relationship with our team mates and team leader.
    We must support each other. We must be dependable to and dependent upon each other's strength, timing and effort, to maximize our effort

as a transparent, synchronized individual member on a team.

God wants us to be successful warfighters, conquering and kicking Satan's butt. He wants us to "rob Hell" and fill Heaven's coffers. He wants us to maximize our effectiveness and efficiency by using His gifts and armor He has already set aside and given to us. It's a two way street.

"Ball's in your court."

Chapter Seven—

Responsibility

Responsibility involves being <u>actively</u> engaged in decision making. Responsibility falls into line with accountability, wherein we have to take account of all our actions prior to and during our assigned mission. Did we train hard enough? Did we encounter any situations requiring more intense preparation? Did we listen and act on the specified orders?

In order to get a better handle on our responsibilities, when combating the spiritual OPFOR, it's necessary to first define and then differentiate between the main elements of human [earthly] combat and spiritual combat.

Human combat operations generally have three categories:

1. Friend: A known entity belonging to the Good Guy force, aka BLUFOR.
2. Hostile: A known entity belonging to the Bad Guys, aka OPFOR.
3. Neutral: An entity that has made a decision (or a non-decision) to not participate; to be a non-combatant; just to observe. To try to ignore the conflict and its potential impacts and consequences. To ride the fence until circumstances change and then lean one way or the other, whichever is then more beneficial.

The Neutral classification, on the initial outset, seems to be the safest position or nomenclature to maintain. However, in many circumstances, a Neutral often will fall into a sub-category called Unknown. When an Unknown enters into an otherwise restricted area of a Shooter, the Unknown can be legitimately killed because its "non-decisive status" can easily turn it into a threat. Being a threat enables Shooters to operate in the modus operandi peculiar to John Wayne, i.e. "Shoot first. Ask questions later."

Spiritual warfare is much simpler to categorize than earthly warfare because there are only two categories. Both categories are combatants! Both are active participants:
1. Believers, aka BLUFOR.
2. Non-believers, aka OPFOR.

Right off the bat, the difference is obvious. There's no Neutral! Where did the Neutrals go? Where's the "None of the above" choice? This doesn't seem to be Politically Correct.

If you believe you can go solo, or just make a non-decision and be a Neutral, you're wrong! Dead wrong. Indecision defaults directly to the Non-believers. It is exactly the same as joining forces with the Non-believer side. It is an unambiguous, no doubt about it "plus" for Satan. There is no riding the rail or straddling the fence in spiritual combat. There's only a "Yes" or "No" position. You is or you isn't. Nothing in between. Satan will use any "non-decision" for his own purposes and benefit. He'll show others how unimportant it is to revere or even consider God as the Commander. He'll use a complacent attitude to reinforce other Non-believers that think in the same [erroneous] manner.

Think about it. If you don't emphatically make a certain choice, then your indecisive, lukewarm, "whatever" decision will be your mark and that will be "your final answer." There's only one choice: Jesus or Satan. You make that choice. You take responsibility for that decision.

God has given you life and an Operations Manual (Ops Manual) to go with it. So many people leave the Ops Manual in the glove compartment. They are content just idling through life. You hear them state: "There's no checklist to follow." "I wish there was a checklist for raising kids, but there isn't. You just got to do your best."

PHT-T-T-T! Hogwash! What a load of politically corrupt crap. Look back to the first sentence of the previous paragraph. God is a responsible God. I'll say it again. God, is a responsible God. He has provided an Ops Manual to guide us in the conduct of our lives.

Let's use a current example to illustrate this point, Ok? It's similar to getting a new car. New as in, "It's new to me" regardless if Johnny, Joe, and Judy have each owned and driven it for 5 years. You ask to see if there's an Owner's Manual and look through it to find out how the heater, a/c, power windows and radio works. How to open the hood, adjust the seats, and get the squirters working for cleaning the windshield. Some of you are reading this and saying, "No way man. I've never done that. I just hop in and go." OK. I admit, some are capable of doing that. But others who choose to operate in that manner still don't know what that stick is in between the seats. They've never pushed on any of the pedals down by their feet. What a nuisance those stupid things are!

They only turn the key, get a herky-jerky start, and are content just idling around at 750 rpm. They have no clue what's under the hood (supercharger, nitrous, or dual quads). They are clueless to the car's capabilities. They can't imagine the thrill they could experience by just pushing on the pedals down by their feet. They are content with what they perceive to be as using all their available faculties. This exemplifies NOT taking responsibility for yourself, for your team, and for NOT using His armor and gifts effectively to accomplish His mission.

I'll admit I haven't seen a specific checklist providing sequential steps for each circumstance encountered while driving a car, and likewise, there isn't a checklist providing each one of us with sequential steps for meeting each moment in our life. But, there sure is a lot of guidance put out about a car's operation and function. For example, if you are in a position to help get a car for your teenager, are you just going to give it to him and let him use it as he pleases? Or do you instruct him about its care, its operation, and the required responsibilities when driving it?

Similarly, God has given you life. Not a materialistic, rust resistant bucket, but LIFE. He has also given you an Ops Manual to live by. He has provided you with the inherent resources to responsibly operate on this earth. Are you responsible enough to learn about the care, operation, and the inherent responsibilities to live, to combat the OPFOR? Are you going to take control of life and learn how to mash the pedals at your feet? Are you going to look down the barrel and pull the trigger, feel the recoil, celebrate in the adrenaline rush? To shout HALLELU-JAH! Whoopee! He's given me a max'ed out life, let me live it to the hilt! Or are you just going to be content and idle along "herky-jerky" and use it until it falls apart?

Chapter Eight—

Discipline

Discipline is a curious word. Everyone knows what discipline means and what it involves. But yet, it's definition and quantitative assessment can be quite vague. Discipline is similar to a moving target, i.e. it's hard to get a bead on it. Therefore, the intent of this section is to de-mystify "discipline," to shine some light on it and to assist in making an objective determination about it. As a combat experienced warfighter this will be beneficial to you, because you'll demand team members that are [based on a quantitative determination] well disciplined.

Let's start at the beginning by asking, "Just what is discipline?" The answer depends upon the type or kind of discipline you desire. No, this is not a trick nor a play on words. Discipline actually has more than one operational meaning. Let's look first at the different forms of discipline. Then illustrate its functional meaning in each form. After that, we should be able to derive its functional application and also be able to assess, quantitatively, its various "states." Ready?

Discipline can be categorized into two different forms:
    Discipline, the noun and
    Discipline, the verb.

A quick aside is required here: Yes, it does irk me to have to admit that my old, crotchety, eighth grade teacher was right... but, "Yes ma'am, I now realize that nouns and verbs are a useful part of our lives."   Gr-r-r-r.

Discipline, The Noun

A noun as most of us recall, is an entity, object, or thing. Most frequently when people think of discipline (the noun) they are referring to a quality of a self-instilled level of motivation, commonly referred to as Self-Discipline.

A classic functional example of Self Discipline is seeing a mountain in the pathway and rather than perceiving it as a daunting obstacle or something to avoid, one notes its usefulness, i.e. "By climbing up its precariously steep side, I'll attain a tactical advantage and see the enemy coming for many miles." Self-Discipline yields fitness in the mental, physical, and spiritual arena. Fitness allows tough circumstances and challenges to be cast aside. Once one starts climbing the mountain, the original "daunting" obstacle reveals a better tactical position and an unobstructed view. This new perception or view increases motivation and enables focus to be kept on the objective, the goal.

Discipline enables the warfighter to keep their eyes on Jesus. When this is maintained, the rocks, obstacles, and distractions in the roadway become meaningless. Keeping fit enables us to hear and listen to His guidance. As we approach closer to God, He draws nearer to us, enabling a distinct point-to-point advantage.

Discipline, The Verb

A verb defines the warfighter's life. It embodies movement, development, and is the purest form of action. The action part of discipline involves correction and guidance. Correction and guidance are the developmental elements that assist the warfighter in changing his mental processing. There are a variety of ways these elements can be administered. Some of the various methodologies include chastisement: to literally beat something into a person or to resort to (administer?) physical blows. Chastisement can also occur in a less abusive form by the use of words. But it can also be used in a positive, reinforcing manner to instruct, correct, reform, reprove, and teach.

Basic Training puts form to the functional definition of discipline. Herein, a new person begins the developmental process toward becoming a warfighter. A wide gamut of teaching "aids" is presented to ensure certain basic principles become natural responses, not requiring thought delays or consideration for implementation. These teaching aids range from the kind guidance given by a caring, father figure (hand on your shoulder, deep caring, solemn cow-eyes) to the standard, negative motivating, raving D.I., "Move! Or you'll find my size 13 in your uncomfortable place!"

Each of these has its place, especially when you consider the obstacle and sense of urgency each motivating style is meant to overcome. For instance, "cow eyes" are not applicable to overcoming life threatening circumstances, but are more closely associated with non-critical, "you'll get the hang of it," there's no-rush, obstacle. On the other hand, a well-placed "threat" from the D.I. (the teacher) directly encourages a sense of urgency to accomplish the action NOW and get it done, exactly right, the first time.

It is essential to understand Jesus' perception of discipline, and just how much our Commander's discipline (noun and verb) is interwoven into our lives. [Digression: Keep this up front in your mind, especially when we progress into Advanced Training. There, we should then be able to more clearly analyze and ascertain whether we are being tested, tempted, or trained.] Back on track: Let's look at several examples when He refers to the various forms of discipline.

#1. Job 36:10a *He also opens their ears for admonition...*

It doesn't take much effort to hear a voice of thunder. Geez Louise. I remember hearing my Gran'ma holler my name down through the valley when she wanted me to fetch something. His voice is much clearer, stronger, and will stop you in your tracks to get your attention.

#2. Rev 3:19 *Those whom I [dearly and tenderly] love,*

This is just like math class. Remember the "if...then" structure?
If X...then Y.
If not X...then no way Y.
This can be rephrased into that mathematical conditional clause: If I care about you, then...

I tell their faults
Basically, here's where you're messing up.

and convict and convince [to them]
He provides us with a rationale that we can accept and take it to heart to understand, and give it a better shot next time.

and reprove and chasten ---
If these are necessary steps to get your attention. If you've really screwed up and He's tired of it. If

you're endangering yourself and others, then this intense form is instituted.

> *[that is] I discipline and instruct them. So be enthusiastic and in earnest and burning with zeal and repent --- changing your mind and attitude.*

Reform comes about when we change our mind. Transformation happens when we change our Spirit, our attitude. Transformation is the execution phase of Reform. It entails acting on your beliefs.

> #3. Prov 3:12 *"For whom the Lord loveth he correcteth; evenso a father the son in whom he delighteth."*

If "Dad" didn't care about you, he would let you run like a wild pig through the woods. But He wants you to succeed, to be an effective, successful warfighter. Therefore, He ensures you are able to wear your armor properly, and shows you how and why to keep your sword sharp. As the Coach is to the players, so the apostles and prophets are to the warfighters.

Heb 12: 5-11 provides us with instructional insight into Jesus' procedural use and reasoning for establishing a disciplined operational environment for warfighters.

> *[5b] ...do not think lightly of the Lord's discipline,*

Let's consider discipline in both of its aspects: noun and verb. As a noun, we can think of Jesus having unflinching discipline. Undeterred by any distractions. Keeping steady regarding right and wrong. As a verb, we can think of Jesus as being our all-knowing leader. His "redirection" provides us with information that we're doing something incorrect, or at least not maximizing our effort. He's not being picky. He's not just toying with us. He's playing hardball because this is an eternally serious business. Therefore, a needed change in focus and perception is required for what He wants us to accomplish NOW.

> *neither become discouraged under His reproof;*

Man, it might seem like we're getting hammered at times, but we're in training, continuously learning. He is paying attention to us, so we need to pay attention to Him. His guidance and redirection are fine-tuning us to become more proficient, powerful, and to stay alive. He's helping us to draw closer to Him to use His gifts more effectively.

> *[6] for the Lord disciplines the person He loves and punishes every son whom He receives."*

If He didn't care about us, He would leave us alone and let us do the headless chicken dance. His punishment, when required, is meant to form a lasting impression so we don't keep making the same [stupid] mistake over, and over, and over, again. We have to suck it up. But it will certainly save our life when we're running point.

> *[7] You must endure for the sake of correction; God is treating you as sons. For what son is there whom the father does not discipline?*

Note the word "must." There's no option here. There's no easy way out. Now, look at "endure". Endure does not mean the time and effort it takes to pull out a splinter from your finger. Do you get

His drift? It's His way or no way. If you don't go through correction and redirection, then you'll soon realize you're NOT on His team. But, Hallelujah! The CINC (Jesus) knows I'm the man to accomplish His mission! Me and Jesus, mano a mano. Come on Satan! We're gonna bust your head.

> *[8] If you receive no correction, such as all sons share,*

Check it out. Everybody on Jesus' team receives direction. We are certainly in no manner perfect, nor can we expect to accomplish any action perfectly. Therefore, He, like our D.I. or coach, grabs our attention and ensures our actions are "refined" for future use. Tell me, how much would your D.I. or coach care about you if he let you go through a drill without telling you where you messed up and how to improve it. How much would he care if he didn't make you do it again…and again…and again… until it was correct?

If you're trained and tasked to defuse explosive devices, you are certainly going to appreciate your instructor for caring and keeping on you, until you get it right. How would you feel if he just gave you a "whatever," "good enough for government work" attitude. I'll tell ya. You wouldn't be feelin' anything after that last big noise…. (Boom!)

> *then you are illegitimate children and not sons.*

Here's the finality, the lasting impact, the end result of the if…then clause. Sons are claimed by Jesus. Illegitimate children are not claimed at all. This is similar to the spiritual combatants' definition of

"Believers" or "Non-Believers". Either or. Sons or cast-outs. You pick. You've seen it many times before. The apron strings are long, or even worse, the umbilical cord was never cut. This is war. There's no "playing nice" or compromising. He cares about you and wants you to be an effective, well-trained warfighter. This is not an easy path. Many are NOT chosen to perform this function.

> *[9] Now if we were corrected by our human fathers and respected them shall we not far rather submit to our spiritual Father and live?*

Who has the best perspective of the battlefield? You or God? If you're truly fighting the battle, then you best keep your eyes where they belong. God is watching the big picture. Keep your eyes on Him because He's got you covered.

> *[10] For while they for a few days disciplined us as they saw fit, He does it for our benefit, so that we may share in His holiness.*

The early American Indians have a proud heritage and trial for becoming a man. A pass/fail trial that is both physically and mentally demanding. Our trial's outcome, as spiritual warfighters, is even greater. Our spiritual "fitness" will determine eternal life or death. If He is going to depend on us, we have to prove ourselves true, and be capable of warring against Satan.

> *[11] Of course, no discipline seems at the time enjoyable,*

No joking here, but it is necessary to refine Tactics, Techniques, and Procedures (TTP) prior to combat. For those who whine through the experience, it is evident they either can't see past their nose or they would just prefer to skate or idle through life.

but it seems painful;
Seems painful? Boy, that's an understatement. But the pain, you've gotta admit is a learning experience. It allows you to get over the next hurdle you come up against. And moreover, the pain is, thankfully, only a short-term effect. Later on, however, discipline affords those schooled in it the peaceful fruitage of an upright life.
Does that surprise you?
.

A lot of you probably thought that Bobby McFerrin made up the lyrics to his song, "Discipline". Or maybe George Washington or some other very wise person probably first said this (verse 11) a couple hundred years ago. That's pretty much correct, in that a very wise person did say this. But the comment is actually older than dirt. Literally, because:
    1. God was the wise person who said this, and
    2. God created dirt.

All right. Now that we've gone through several examples, you're thinking they all say the same thing. Duh-h! You're absolutely right. How many times, in how many ways, does He have to say it? To get it through that rock-hard head? He's laying it out for you. What's the problem?
    Enough said.

Chapter Nine—

Vigilance

> 1Thes 5:6 *So then, let us not be asleep like the rest, but let us be on our guard and be sober.*

It takes discipline to not fall into the trap of peer pressure or for taking the easy way out.

> 1Pet 5:8 *Exercise self-control. Be on your guard. Your opponent, the devil prowls around like a roaring lion in search of someone to devour. [9] Firm in your faith, resist him, aware that throughout the world, sufferings of this kind are imposed upon your brothers.*

During the writing of these letters from the Supreme Commander, Paul (1 Thes.) and Peter (1 Pet.) both express a concern for vigilance. I can see Jesus dictating the letter to Paul in 50 AD: "Paul, we've got to tell the people it's important to remain on guard at all times. They didn't understand it when I told Cain back in Genesis 4:7 that "*if you do not do what is right, sin* (an acronym for Stinking Satan Is Near) *is crouching at your door; it desires to have you, but you must master it.*" So, take down the following…"

And then about 15 years later, God notices the message evidently still wasn't understood because of ongoing actions from His children. Therefore, He tells Peter: "I can see y'all are having difficulty in [not] dealing with that stinkin' Satan. Peter, take this down. I'm going to make it absolutely clear!"

When God addresses the same topic twice, and the second time emphasizes with great specificity the imminent danger that rogue colonel and his OPFOR present, we need to realize this is NOT a matter to take lightly. We need to take this to heart! If the CINC foot stomps this instruction, it's adamant we put it up front in our Ops Manual as a Warning.

For those of you unfamiliar with the severity of a Warning in a Technical Manual, there are three different categories of awareness: Note, Caution, and Warning. A Note presents "neat to know" information, but one can just as easily blow over it without suffering any negative impact. A Caution informs the technician that attention to this detail is warranted. And then the Warning is given when actual danger is present and loss of life can occur.

Take great regard in acknowledging the lion is looking for some ONE to maul, to devour, to maim or kill. Not some THING. Not an inanimate object, or another beast in the wilderness. He's looking. Correction. He's hunting. Wantonly to chew you up, to permanently cripple and disable you from fighting him anymore.

Sometimes this is a tough nut for humans to crack. There is a living, breathing evil spirit out there preying for your moment of weakness. It will seize upon that physical, emotional, or spiritual moment without hesitation.

What can you do to protect yourself? Check out verse 9: Stand firm. Resist him! Maintain your SA. Blow the bugle, sound the alarm, fire the flare. Call out the name of Jehovah Nissi (the Conqueror)! This is a mandatory checklist. It requires adherence. These are commands. Verbal in-your-face orders given to you, His troops, in preparation for battle.

Chapter Ten—

Discipleship

I just wanted to address this topic briefly. Briefly, not because it's not important but rather because it enables one to realize there are going to be differences in the warrior rank and file, e.g. Seaman – Admiral and Airman/Private – General. A spiritual category or rank exists for those proven in combat and deemed to be honored as "Disciples".

Let's lock in our focus by defining "disciple". Disciple:
- a pupil, a student,
- one who invests time and effort to listen and learn
- a helper, a supporter
- an advocate.

Did you notice the vast amount of difference or implied differences between a pupil and a student? Which requires more dedicated intensity? I know I was a student in high school. I'd prefer not to divulge what activities I was a student of, but you get the idea.

I didn't really become a pupil until I took my first course in Mandarin Chinese. The language just grabbed my whole, complete, undistracted attention. It consumed my life and total interest. I couldn't learn enough about the Chinese language, history, food, culture, etc. That is what being a pupil means. Keeping our eyes focused, literally.

We've all invested time, money, and effort into things. Why? Because we expect a payoff later on down the road. In regards to money we ask, "What's the Return on Investment (ROI) going to be? What's the yield?" In spiritual matters, the investment is self-subordination, self-sacrifice. "What's in it for me?" The ability to clearly hear and understand the CINC; to be an effective warfighter on His team.

A helper primarily lends time and physical effort. A helper probably doesn't make influential decisions and doesn't necessarily have to be really committed to the cause. However, a supporter assists in efforts both mentally and physically. Commitment is part and parcel to the aid package provided.

An advocate takes part in all levels of activities noted above. Plus, an advocate takes action, verbally and physically, to ensure the action is completed effectively, efficiently and with lasting surety.

Manner and degree is a key differentiating factor in being a disciple. This manner and degree makes it easy to understand why there is a rank and file among warfighters. I need to reiterate that age is <u>not</u> a differentiating factor in the process for determining the rank and file of warfighters and disciples. Teaching the apostolic foundations and supernatural gifts, and wearing the armor the CINC has given us needs to occur at an early "age." Each warfighter needs to determine and use these capabilities as soon as possible.

Warm milk is meant for babies. Slapping heavy steaks on a grille is meant for mature people. It's really uncomfortable (and downright wrong!) to watch a 20 year old Christian still sucking warm milk out of a bottle.

To close the loop, it would be a good idea to come up with an operational definition for "disciple". How about:

Truly tried, tested, experienced, enlightened, confident, enduring, faithful warfighter.

Scarred, scratched, combat oriented, completely focused.

Master of sword sharpening, flag raising, and rescue.

An expert in Plans, Strategies, Laying foundations, and determining timing for synchronized combat operation.

On Satan's Top 10 Most Wanted List!

Hooah!

Living, breathing examples of disciples would be the apostles and prophets that are helping war the good war today. They challenge old tactics, techniques, and procedures to ensure they are still effective in accomplishing God's current Operations. They are also able to reveal and develop current plans and strategies based on the Commander's Initial Priority Targeting List.

Given these inputs, our leaders are better prepared to assign the warfighter's their sectors, stake out perimeters, and ensure the foundations are secure before the actual battle(s) begin. This kind of Intel causes us to look forward to the upcoming battle and accomplishing His mission.

Only those who follow and act according to His words will be honored by the role and title of Disciple. God has given us the Rules of Engagement (ROE) and provided many detailed checklists to ensure we accomplish His will. He has also provided us with what I call His Congressional Medal of Honor speech. To be awarded the

Congressional Medal of Honor by the President of the United States is a rare and truly honorable event. To be awarded this by God is... I'm deprived of any words to properly describe this honor.

Congressional Medal of Honor

Romans 12:1a "...*in view of God's mercies, present your bodies as a living sacrifice*,
Sacrifice: the act; the victim, literally. Sacrifice: the epitome or ultimate giving, releasing control. Submitting, subordinating all mental, physical, and spiritual entities to Him for His use, direction, and repair.

When you desire to give your all to Him, that's what it means. Allowing Him to use His power to give you direction and capabilities to complete His [perfect] will. A complete turnover: mental, physical, emotional, spiritual, material, designated and delegated power and authorities. Everything. Complete. No exceptions; no holdbacks. No reservations.

[1b] *holy and acceptable to God, which is your reasonable [logical] service.*"
Sacrificing our personal life is acceptable to God? Does He really expect this? Or is He just playing hardball with us? Is it really reasonable for God to expect this from each one of us? [Dedicated warfighter or sheep?] Let's look at this in the proper perspective. He did sacrifice His only son. How can we claim to be more important than Jesus? His only son. Is this expectation unreasonable?

Minimum demands for true discipleship (discipline?):

Luke 14:33 *Whosoever he be of you that **forsake**th not all that he hath*
Literally each of us who can't part with all his earthly possessions,

cannot be my disciple.
Is this a simple, factual, no questions left statement, or what? We, as warfighters, must recognize our bankruptcy. Bankruptcy denotes not only a huge financial loss requiring a complete reorganization of procedures, communication, etc, in the personal life, but He is also talking about bankruptcy in our physical, emotional, and mental life as well.

This one word is doing its best to depict a down and out realization that we are nothing (absolutely nothing) more than a dying, decomposing shell without Him. Once we invite Him in, we become living beings with a Spirit, a purpose. The realization that our life is actually His life. He is the core of our body, being, mind, soul, and spirit. Thereafter, we need to be, act, think, hear and listen to what He wants us to do. His will. His plan. His credit.

This is one of the first steps in being a disciple, i.e. discipline. Synchro-congruent. Our sole wealth is vested in the One whom God has credited to him in the person and by the presence of His divine Spirit.

Now back to Romans 12:2

> "And do not conform to the present world system, but be transformed by the renewal of your mind, so as to sense for yourselves what is the good and acceptable and perfect will of God."

Here Paul further delineates the requirement from God. Basically, he's stating to use your mind and new [reformed] focus on Jesus to deal with the environment we are currently experiencing. Then, with our special training [which reinforces our assigned expertise, i.e. AFSC, MOS] we can then determine the mission. We can execute our reformed training and do [transform], act on, what is acceptable to God's perfect will.

Disciple. Do you have what it takes? Are you a contender?

Chapter Eleven—

Advanced Training

You've passed the Initial Qualifying Tests. Looking back at Basic Training, there were some [seemingly] high hurdles that were tough to clear, but you did it. You're selected for graduate training. Your body and mind are tried [and probably tired] and tested. Advanced Training is another step in the building block process. Advanced Training will refine and hone the basic skills you've now acquired. It will be tougher, more rewarding, and you will be one step closer to actually having the opportunity to engage the enemy from a tactically advantageous threshold (Jesus' side). Are you ready to proceed? If so, you will continue to put your mind and body to the test, strengthening them, while simultaneously finding out the content of your soul and spirit. This is, afterall, the reason you volunteered for this mission. To please God. To search Him out. To find out the truth that resides in your soul.

Up to this point, we've been discussing required changes in the individual's mental attitude, mental processing and perception. We've progressed from a self-centered view to keeping our eyes focused on our leader and team members. The progression nominally advanced through the following steps:

1. Self-motivation: confident, energetic, active, vigorous. Growth directly correlates to closeness to God, i.e. the closer we draw near to

God, the greater our motivation and the more vigorous our pursuit.

    2. Self-discipline: strength in mind, will, and determination. Continuous refinement via training.

    3. Team-spirit: commonality, shared goals, cohesion, camaraderie. This is the beginning of progressing from reform (our newfound perception) to transform (acting on our reformed processing with all our heart and spirit).

    4. Team discipline: control, obedience, authority. To interdependently maneuver and flex, in sync, to an operational environment that constantly poses new situations, and encounters new [unexpected] variables.

    5. Team responsibility: dependable, reliable, trustworthy. Loyal subordination of self to the CINC's goals and objectives ensures team synergies. Maximizes team effectiveness in executing His orders.

Now that the basic fundamentals of individual development have been trained, and the concepts of teamwork have been addressed, it's time to begin a required phased/stepped process to ensure team integrity under trying, stressful, combative conditions. But note after the initial entry levels are completed, the steps loop back for further refinement, and drawing even nearer to God.

Advanced Training is meant to be a tough process. It is an extended up front, in-your-face readjustment of values. Therefore, it requires a lot of discipline to accomplish the needed refocus, redirection, the learning of new skills and how to effectively integrate our actions with other team members.

This shift in mental, physical, and spiritual priorities can seem to be very punishing. However, it is not punishment. It is actually strengthening us to execute our orders, to effectively engage the enemy. Advanced Training ensures readiness for action. It keeps us focused on the mission and enables us to adapt to changes in the enemy's tactics.

Advanced Training requires one's actions or feats to be openly exposed. It reveals to everyone, the strengths and weaknesses of each individual as they undergo physical and mental challenges and stress. Each team member not only becomes intimately cognizant of his own capabilities (and lack thereof), but also cognizant of each teammates' capabilities.

The axiom that the whole team is only as strong as its weakest link does NOT apply to a well-trained team. Team discipline and responsibility bear on each individual team member, but team strength can follow a logarithmic rise when even one member acts as a catalyst (Hooah!). This can push/pull each member over and beyond their own personal, normally "weak" threshold.

Paul provides a God-given procedural checklist that explicitly details for His warfighters how to train to overcome this man-inspired "weak link" theory. Check it out:

> 1Thes 5:11 *Encourage one another. Build up one another*

Motivation! A high five. Come on. Don't stop, just one more! Push past the pain. Semper Fi!

> *[12] We beg of you, brothers, to recognize the workers among you, those who are leaders in the Lord and your advisers.*

Leadership. Whoever has the skill, enable/help them to accomplish what's required to maximize the team effort and timeliness to succeed. Heed those who give wise counsel from the CINC.

> *[13] Because of their work, hold them lovingly in highest regard. Enjoy peace among yourselves.*

Hey, for leaders who have proven themselves, we need good followers. In many circumstances, leadership is a transient, fluid entity, moving from one team member to another as the encountered task demands. Sincere, caring, enthusiastic support will bolster the team's energy and also create a "hardening bond" (a catalyst for a solid foundation) between members.

> *[14] But,*

This is a Caution; if not at times a Warning! Read and absorb the following:

> *we appeal to you, brothers: warn the idle, encourage the faint-hearted, give your support to the weak, exercise patience toward everyone.*

Ok, everyone isn't meant to be a warfighter or shooter. We, warfighters, still need to tell these people the Truth and the consequences of their [non]decisions. Others need to be grabbed by the arm (not the neck), and still others need to be transported immediately on our shoulders out of the danger zone. We'll reconcile their weaknesses later, during a less critical moment.

> *[17] Pray unceasingly.*

Keep your leader, Jesus, informed of significant events, upcoming challenges, signs of weakness,

RFWs (Requests For Wisdom), and give praise for His armor.

> *[19] Do not stifle the Spirit.*

Don't be concerned with what non-believers think or even of what believing "wannabes" think. If the Holy Spirit directs you to do something, then...
Grunt. Push harder. **SHOUT** for joy! Don't be a slacker. No whine and cheese served here. Semper Fi!

> *[21] Do not despise prophetic utterance,*

Don't automatically castigate the Intel guys.

> *[21] but test it all and retain what is good.*

Performance-based decision making. If the CEP is tight, use it. Make sense?

> *[22] Keep away from evil in every form.*

Here's another emphatic statement. Simplified for those who require cartoons. This ensures there is no question left hanging; there's no doubt about it...DON'T become one with the enemy. Do NOT become indistinguishable from the enemy. Stand apart! This can be difficult in today's world.

On earth, we've given our previously designated enemies, our most friendly, favored nation status. Becoming Politically Correct has certainly smeared the once distinguishable black and white, into a pool of gray.

Jesus does want us to love our brothers and enemies, even as they go astray. However, we are still obligated to stand tall for what is required of us, as warfighters for Him. There is NO compromise on this point. Either we are on His side or not. It's "Yes" or "No". Don't be the "casualty" requiring a Combat Search and Rescue (CSAR) and putting the other members of your team in jeopardy unnecessarily. Keep away from the enemy. This is especially important during Basic Training. He (Satan) knows your [high] spirits, your good intentions, and your desire to do what's right for God. However, your strength and endurance might not yet be ready to do direct battle with a prepared, professional, experienced opponent.

> 2Pet 2:19 *While they promise liberty*

Peace, understanding, i.e. why can't we all just get along, Rodney?

> *they are themselves slaves of corruption...*

High falutin' ideas, but they can't see past the despotic nose on their face.
Furthermore, ... remember that if...then clause? Here it comes:

> *[20] if those who have escaped the contaminations of the world through the knowledge of Jesus, are again entangled and overcome by them,*

> then

BOOM!

> *their last condition becomes worse than the first.*

This is self-explanatory. If you succumb to the world [again], you're gonna be sucking stale air.

Chapter Twelve—

Specialty Skills

An effective team has numerous members that can perform a wide variety of specialties, i.e. experts in their own field. For example, on a football team, we don't want everyone to be a Center. Everyone can't be a quarterback either, because someone needs to catch the ball and run, and others need to protect the quarterback by blocking.

In combat ops the requirement for diversity in background reminds me of the movie, <u>The Dirty Dozen</u>, wherein a group of lawless individuals were selected. Brought out from prison during WWII, they volunteered to accomplish a high-risk mission whereupon the survivors would have their freedom granted. These people (brigands and rogues) were bound together for a single purpose.

Similarly, we too are volunteers to a chosen group of warfighters. Bound together for one ultimate purpose, wanting to be faithful to our leader's (Jesus) direction in order to be set free.

The Dirty Dozen recognized two distinct facts: (1) They had to operate as a team and (2) they had to follow (be faithful to) their leader's orders for any of them to survive and become free. Each of the soldiers had a different purpose to fulfill. Some were assigned unique tasks (Eph 4:11), while others worked within the larger team.

I Corinthians 12:18 *But now hath God set the members every one of them in the body, as it hath pleased Him.*

God wants each one of us to accomplish the task we are assigned. The task (read "task" as using a special God-given gift) is already there. God is waiting for us to execute His order. We need to listen, observe, and then act upon it, to accomplish His purpose.

Whoops, let me digress a minute here. "Observe" needs to be defined as, intently studying the complete Ops Environment. Observe is not casually sitting on the front porch with a glass of cold lemonade and watching the grass grow. If you have difficulty in differentiating between multi-syllabic words, think of "observe" as "Watch". Watch, like a Guard Dog! Ears, eyes, nose, all senses on high alert. Watch-ing his assigned environment.

Back on track: Not a task assigned by man, and especially not one we, ourselves, as puny humans want to do. But He has a specific, special purpose for each one of us. Rather than managing us as individual, autonomous "stovepipes" (as non-warfighters attempt to run their own lives), God (the CINC/JFC) coordinates activities with orderly, synchronized fulfillment for His purpose. Each person is a member of a team, committed to a particular purpose. TEAMwork.

How do you find out what special gifts God has already given you? Do you just go out and do something? After all, I just finished saying action is a key principle. So are you going to be active: Like a puppy enthusiastically chasing its tail? Like a fighter jet in full thrust, but without vector? Or do you pause, read, pray, contemplate, talk with other leaders, hear what is said, and listen. Not just hear;

but listen. Listening entails a two-way communication between one who is speaking and the other who is actively participating in the conversation, but in a receive mode.

For example, a farmer knows exactly what to expect from a certain type of seed. But before it is planted in the ground, the ground must first be prepared. So it is with warfighters. Listen to the leader (apostle/pastor/prophet). Talk with Him/them. Enable them to reveal your capabilities. Allow them to provide you with input: specific direction, encouragement, prophetic words, etc. Absorb this information to prepare yourself to listen, personally. God is already speaking. Can you hear Him? Are you listening with all your heart and soul? Are you totally focused?

After the ground and weather conditions are correct, then and only then does the ground receive the seed from the farmer. With continued nourishment and care, growth ensues. Likewise, only when you're physically and mentally prepared will you receive (perceive) your gift from God.

Continued nourishment (praying continuously) is necessary for growth to follow. Prayer comes in many forms (thinking, praising, singing, meditating, etc.), but the ultimate overarching condition is focus. Focus on Jesus. Maintain your physical eyes and the eyes of your heart on Him.

Focus is succinctly summed up in:

Psalms 119:10a *Seek the Lord with your whole heart*

In order to accomplish this search, we have to personalize our life for Jesus. A concerted, focused, unconditional effort. By keeping our focus, we'll avoid and out-maneuver many temptations, road hazards, ambushes, and land mines along the trail. Following in the point man's footsteps ensures safety and requires discipline. Remember it sounds and looks easy. But then, why doesn't everyone just follow in His footsteps? Simple answer: Discipline. Desire. Training.

>1Pet 4:10 *God has given each of you some special abilities*

We see these everyday in the sports world: baseball players, golfers, track stars, all breaking records set by their predecessors. If this is happening in "man's" world, how much greater is the potential in "God's" world? Don't guess on this one. Let me tell you. He has called some to be Prophets and Apostles. You can see them in human form, everyday. They are the ones who:
  -Provide direction.
  -Offer themselves as a source of confirmation in the timing and placement of Plans & Strategies, as well as warfighters.
  -Impart spiritual gifts and reveal current truths.
  -Take the stand of being a true warrior.
  -Build teams, secure the perimeter, and establish base camps to operate from.
Are these your gifts too? Have you opened them, yet? We need to find out what our gifts are so we can...

>*be sure to use them*

I can't say whether this was actually meant to be a warning or not. But I know when my Dad or Gran'ma used to look at me and say, "Be sure you..." In Lower Alabaman vernacular, what this really means is: "Rich, ensure you do NOT screw this up!" I knew without a doubt, we were dealing in serious business. There was no room for bartering or miscalculation. If I didn't hold up my part of the action, there would be a serious reckoning in the very near future.

Consider this also. You give someone a birthday gift, and return next year for their birthday party again, with another gift. But, you notice they haven't even opened your first gift, yet. What are you going to think? What are you going to do? I believe God acts in the same manner. How can He give us more power, authority and supernatural gifts, if we don't open them up and use them?!?

Don't try and give Him any lame excuses like, "I didn't know I had that gift." Or "What am I s'posed to do with it?" Get in the Ops Manual, talk with your leaders, seek counsel from the apostles and prophets. And continue to be aware when the Commander, God, says, "[You] Be sure _you_ use them…" Because He is serious about it!

to help each other

Not for profit and not for inflating your own ego. Use them [God-given abilities/talents] to help each other. This is not rocket science. It's a simple declarative. A command. It's a fact, Jack.

passing on to others God's many kinds of blessings.

How do you pass God's blessings around to others? Come on. Give me a break. How do you pass a football around? You grab it and throw it away. You hand it off or give it to someone else. You certainly don't hold onto it for yourself. The more times you throw it to someone else, what happens? It keeps coming back. For you chair ridden quarterbacks, we call this "passing the football around." OK? Now, tell me what's so different about passing God's blessings around?

[11] Are you called to preach? Then preach
What did the coach always say? Do you know how to run that play? Then DO IT!!! If God has given you the ability to heal people and you don't use it... You keep it to yourself and watch people continue to hobble around in spiritual and physical pain... That's not a good thing.

By not acting, it is a criminal act. You want to play hardball? I'll tell you something else. Each of us has the ability to "give" eternal life. By speaking the Truth. If we keep this internal, to ourself... If we don't act, who is responsible for the killing? Who is the criminal? That's a hardcore perspective on my part and it won't set easy with some of y'all. But think about it.

I'm most thankful that God is merciful, for I believe he's trying to be patient with us. He could just as easily have said: "HEY, can you preach? Then DO IT!" End of statement. Period. Dot. No questions. Just do it!

as though God Himself were speaking through you.
You'll have no option BUT to speak with authority. Be BOLD. Be STRONG. Fear NOT. Make no qualms about it. This is God's gift to you. Don't be some two-headed, snake in the grass, bureaucratic politician, fearful of alienating someone by speaking the straight up truth. His Spirit will fill your mouth with His words. Just DO it.

Are you called to help others?
Then get off your butt and Do It!

> *Do it with all the strength and energy that God supplies,*

Unlike us weak, good-intentioned humans, God's strength is never waning, never fading, and never susceptible to becoming tired. It is immeasurable.

> *so that God will be glorified through Jesus Christ--to Him be glory and power forever and ever.*

We need to tap into His power meter. His glory is reflected by the glow, the power surge He gives us.

> *Amen.*

You've got two options here. (1) Fast forward to the Amen section or (2) Be sure you.... remember this when you get to the Amen section.

> 1Tim 4:14 *Be sure to*

Wow. Here it is again. Tell me. When the Commander says the same thing more than once, is it important? Is it a foot stomper? Or are the students just a little on the dense side?

> *use the abilities God has given you*

Hello! This is not a suggestion. This is NOT a recommendation. This is a requirement, a mandate. Let's make it real easy to understand. "Use 'em! Or lose 'em."

> *through His prophets when the elders of the church laid their hands upon your head.*

Yes, prophets, like elders, exist even today. Prophets and apostles are used to reinforce and clarify His message to us warfighters.

[15] Put these abilities to work; throw yourself into your tasks so that everyone may notice your improvement and progress.
Train, train, train. Transform the candle into a laser. Let your light shine. Afterall, you are serving as a conduit for His light.

[16] Keep a close watch on all you do
Be on alert. Watch! Self- and TEAM-discipline is a must.

and think
No excuses! Use your head. Keep the bolts on your neck tight. Extreme discipline is required for this. The mind feeds the body. The body displays the actions fed by the brain. There's a "loop" here. One feeds the other. Don't let any part become corrupted.

Stay true to what is right
There's black, and then there's white.
There's believers, and then there's non-believers.
There's right, and then there's wrong.
Staying true means staying on target with His [directional] will. NOT riding on the ragged edge. NOT straying off into the politically correct greyness. NOT having to define what "is" is.

and God will bless you and use you to help others.
Here's that "loop" again. Remember throwing the football? You toss it to someone and, lo and behold, it gets tossed back to you for more action. This God-centered life-style is a loop, a complex interwoven, multi-nodal inter-connecting, interdependent network. Warfighters helping others, helping other warfighters.... helping others.

Chapter Thirteen—

Testing

We're tested for promotion; tested for proficiency; tested for durability; tested for standardization. Shoot, we're even tested [for blood] when we're sicker than a dog or at the peak of fitness. So what's all the fuss about testing?

Many think that taking a test negatively motivates people to improve. Sometimes it is a negative motivating force that pushes us on. A desire to stay up with our classmates, team members, etc., to not be left behind. Speaking of behind, I remember my D.I. with the size 13 boots. Now, he [his active foot] was a motivator. Behind. Never be behind.

> Testing defined:
> 1Pet 1:7 *so that the testing of your faith, far more precious than perishable gold that is tested by fire, may prove to be for praise and glory and honor when Jesus Christ is revealed.*

If the hunk of our faith/"gold" isn't tested, it will remain just that. Just a hunk of gold. Without testing there are just too many unknowns, too many potential impurities mixed within to make a [ap]praiseworthy statement about it.

So we are as Christian warfighters. The testing of our faith rids us of any impurities. The resulting successful emergence after the testing period (the battle we wage with God right at our side) will prove to make us noteworthy for praise, glory, and honor. If we don't allow a test to occur, our indecision turns out to be our decision. We remain just conglomerate rock with only pieces of God's gold, or is it feldspar? Difficult to tell without testing it, aye? God is calling. Are you listening? What is your answer?

Hang on to your hat, because this is just my personal perception. Although I believe you'll find it has merit. OK? Testing exposes our current level of readiness [skill, confidence, attitude, desire, and willingness] to our CINC, to our team members and to ourselves. The results readily reveal the current level of our strengths, weaknesses, and whether we're ready for the next step of responsibility, power, or engagement for combat.

Testing is a necessary element for advancement and promotion. Remember! Spiritual warfighters are assessed, aka tested, via a performance-based system. Therefore, when the going gets tough or seems to be getting treacherous, keep your focus. Focus requires discipline and the CINC rewards discipline. So, reach out to Him. He won't push us past our limit.

Chapter Fourteen—

Trials

Testing and trials seem to be synonymous terms. But even synonyms vary in manner and degree. In combat, the difference between testing and trials is not only in manner and degree, but also in intensity. Recognizing the differences between these terms will help the warfighter identify the type of encounter he's facing, i.e. a single "sniper" event vs. a low intensity conflict vs. a declared war.

A test can generally be considered a single event. We all know from school that even a test can differ in time, duration, and intensity. For example, different types of tests can range the gamut from pop quizzes to midterms to comprehensive dissertations for an advanced degree. Time, intensity, and duration are identifiably and significantly different in these examples. You can shrug the pop quiz off as an annoyance at times, but the "comps" can potentially wear and tear at you for months.

A trial involves an even greater length of time and intensity than a test. Endurance is definitely a factor in overcoming a trial successfully. Furthermore, the outcome from enduring a trial has much greater consequences. What happens at the end of a trial? The Judge makes one decision. In spiritual combat, the decision is either "Worthy" or "Not Worthy" [needs more work]. Let's see what our Leader has to say about Trials to ensure we're on track.

> Heb 10:36 *For you need endurance...*

How do we become long distance warfighters? In sports and weight training, as well as in spiritual growth, endurance only comes by the physical breakdown of muscle tissue, accomplished by a progressive overloading of the muscle. We've heard it before: "No pain, no gain." In order to reach our aerobic max, we must also go through anaerobic troughs.

Endurance doesn't just happen. Training, focus, practice, sacrifice, tension (physical, mental, and spiritual), teamwork (advanced concepts of fundamental applications) requires greater energy, but enables greater gains and rewards. Discipline is instilled. Hearing begins to tend toward listening. Can you "hear" His voice, yet?

> *to gain the promised blessing upon accomplishing what God wills.*

This is the goal. To hear, listen, understand, and then execute exactly what the Commander wants. To be in constant communication with Him; to respond immediately when tasked.

> *[38] but he whom I find righteous through faith*

He that has endurance, who stays true to the course, who executes the plan accordingly.

> *will live,*

God gives you the opportunity to don his armor and to employ weapons against the enemy successfully.

and if he shrinks, back,
Listen up! Here comes one of those "if...then" clauses: *If he shrinks back* Especially after God has instructed, taught, and trained you. Then "OUCH"...

My soul
Not His emotions. Not His mind. Not His temperament, but His **soul**. Deep down inside, the core of Jesus' being.

will not be pleased with him.
This is NOT a good thing! This is what separates the warfighters from the wannabes. Execution. Anyone can study the plan. Listen to the instructor. Say the words. Go through practices and training. But this is when the rubber meets the road. When you're standing face-to-face, toe-to-toe with Satan, if you blink, hesitate or are late in firing, collateral damage, loss of life to you, your teammates, and to your position will result. This is the ultimate test to show God your faith in action. Are you a descendent of Abraham? Then act like it or get out of the way!

[39] However,
Man, cast off that negative-wave thinking before engaging the enemy. You're gonna kick his butt and you know it!

WE
Note the specificity of this remark: "We". We equals you, me, and Jesus; You and Jesus; Jesus and I; we'uns, y'uns, y'all and Jesus. There's no "mystery mouse" involved here. Like when my Dad said, "Rich, we're gonna cut the grass today." How could "we" do this when "we" only had one lawn mower

and I was gonna ride my dirt bike in the woods today?
Uh-huh.
Let's continue:

> **WE ARE NOT** *of those who shrink back so as to perish*

God will NOT allow [fear] this to happen to our team. He will NOT allow His warriors to spiritually die. Put a mental picture of this in your mind. Have you ever heard thunder just rolling across the skies? This was the exact sound of His voice when He spoke this command. A resounding voice of thunder; spoken by a tongue sharper than any two-edged sword. This **IS** a rousing battle cry for strength and endurance to <u>all</u> warfighters!

> *but of those who have faith and save their souls.*

Right on, Lord! We're putting our faith into action to combat evil. To save not only our own souls, but also those of our teammates and those who need to be snatched out of the fire! Knockin' heads, kickin' butt, takin' names. Satan, yours is first!

> James 1:2 *Consider it complete joy, my brothers, when you become involved in all sorts of trials,*

Go ahead, put notches in your gun belt! When the judge slams the gavel down and shouts, "Well deserved, faithful "warring" servant!" You'll know complete joy.

> *[3] well aware that the testing of your faith brings out steadfastness.*

Steadfastness, endurance, dedication, discipline. When the going gets tough, warfighters are there to answer the call, to assist fellow warfighters and others in fighting battles toe-to-toe.

> *[4] But let steadfastness have full play, so that you may be completed and rounded out with no defects whatever.*

No pain, no gain. Tried, tested, and true. That is the composite sketch of a faithful warfighter. Here's your chance to graduate from the Dirty Dozen. Complete freedom and pure satisfaction are yours now and forevermore.

> James 1:12 *Blessed is the man who stands up under trial; for when he has stood the test, he will receive the crown of life that God has promised to those who love Him.*

The ultimate reward, the [Heavenly] Congressional Medal of Honor. Discipleship. You must earn it. Even Jesus was tested. He had to put up with the weakness of the flesh for 33 years. He could have, at any time called upon His Father or angels to put Him back in His rightful place in heaven. But He didn't. He was steadfast in His position. He was true to the course.

But how does one identify whether they are currently undergoing a test, a trial, or being subjected to temptation? Although I don't believe there is a hard and fast rule to provide positive ID on each one. There is a good rule of thumb we can apply. Ready?

Here's the big difference between a test, a trial and a temptation. Tests and trials can be tough events or sequences of events that really puts one's discipline and spirit to work. Temptation on the other hand has a twist. It has a base of sin. The "Spin Doctor" [see Glossary] would say these are the same things; they're just "perfunctory" synonyms. Don't get caught in this crock. God says,

> *[13] Let no one who is tempted say, "I am tempted by God," for God cannot be tempted by evil and He tempts no one.*

That is a promise!

> *[14] But each person is tempted when he is drawn away and enticed by his own desire.*

There's the twist. Do NOT cut the Spin Doctor any slack. Do NOT listen to him; he is death in disguise.

> *[15] Then when the desire has conceived it gives birth to sin, and sin, when it reaches maturity, produces death.*

Hate to say it, but I told ya! Temptation is the fight between the weakness of the flesh and the trueness of the Holy Spirit. Stay true. Don't let a [seemingly] inconsequential scratch [i.e. a weakness] develop into a severe, debilitating wound.

Chapter Fifteen—

Suffering aka Grit, Spit, & G'it

Suffering might seem to fall in the same category as Testing and Trials. It could be a sub-category of either one of them. However, I earnestly believe it needs its own category. If not, then it needs to be co-located in the proximity of discipleship, as a minimum. However, to preclude any arguments [and because I'm writing this book, not you], I've decided to address it here to maintain a logical thought process. "Just be sure" you recall it from your database when re-reading the Disciple section.

We all acknowledge Suffering is the extreme form of Testing and Trials. It's way out on the end of the stick; on the skewed end of a bell curve. It's bad news, physically, emotionally, psychologically, and [potentially] spiritually to the victim. From the observers viewpoint.

What? Does that sound like a catch? Is this a hook with a juicy plastic worm on it? Heh, heh, heh. "Come on in, the waters fine!" said my blue friend to me. Misery loves company.

Let's look at, and for Suffering. Suffering is associated with some really harsh, nerve-racking synonyms: agony, tribulations, anguish, torment, affliction. It exudes pure, utterly indescribable pain, in its most acute form.

Let's jump right to the source to find out His plan for those who are, or are about to suffer. We need to know the ROE. We need to be able to keep our focus when we're getting wracked and stacked by the OPFOR!

> 1Pet 3:17 *For it is better, if it is God's will, to suffer for doing right than for doing wrong.*
> 1Pet 4:12 *Do not be surprised, dear friends, at the fiery test that is coming upon you, as if you were experiencing something unheard of. [13] Instead, be joyful that you are sharing to some degree the sufferings of Christ, in order that at the revealing of His glory you may be full of joy. [14] If you are defamed for the name of Christ, you are blessed, because the Spirit of glory, yes, the Spirit of God, is resting on you. [16] but if you suffer as a Christian, do not be ashamed, but praise God because you bear that name. [19] For this reason let those who are suffering according to the will of God entrust their souls to God, the faithful Creator, while they do what is right.*

No further clarification, explanation or pontification is required. The CINC said it specifically enough. However, I would like to bounce my own perception of suffering off of you, my team members. This is caveated "Conant" so go find the salt shaker, Ok?

I've gone through some pretty horrific training. But I know people who have gone through worse. I'd like to put their names up in lights for their 15 seconds of fame before I start.

SEALs, PJs, Delta Force, and the other unnamable, unsung heroes, we salute you for your earthly discipline and suffering.

Ok, let's press on.

What is it about these Special Operations names that invoke mental perceptions of suffering?

We've heard the stories and seen the Discovery channel's exposé on their training "aids" and techniques. We suffer with them in their agony. Right?

This is where, I believe [invoke the Conant caveat now], that suffering is on the most part, the perception from the observer sitting on the bleachers; sitting on the sideline, and affixed on the couch. Suffering is an observable trait, assessed and subjectively quantified by the non-active, non-participating, wannabe warfighter, watching the combat engagement from a remotely distant display. To the active warring, direct combatant, there is no current suffering.

What?

How can I say that?

I'm able and fully confident in stating that because I know under dire circumstances, when the rubber is hot on the road, there is NO time to even think about suffering. (Excuse the improper English, but it's meant to provide absolute, emphatic, factual emphasis!) In combat ops, when the warfighter is hunkered down, and all that comes out is blood, sweat, and grunts.... It's all about winning. About living. No time to think about dieing. That's the OPFORs job. Mano a mano. Me & Jesus vs Satan. It's all about territorial [spiritual and physical] conquering. Attaining objectives. Overpowering weak spots in the enemy.

Attack!

Counter!

Thrust!

Attack, Attack, ATTACK!

This is pure excitement. Satisfaction and joy happen later on, when the body slows down and the brain becomes re-engaged. We didn't "suffer" to get the job done. We hunkered down, grunted, groaned, shouldered the weight and pushed through (with Jesus) to conquer and overcome.

Suffer? Nah!

Fight? You bet! Constantly. Forever.

It's true. We're not able to hide the battle scars on our face and body. We'll take some hits; lose some blood; crack some bones. We won't have the prettiest dental display. But we WILL be victorious. These are notches in our gun belt. Our medals of honor, earned not purchased. Be proud. Be bold. We're strong.

The question was asked in Discipleship, "What's the Return On Investment?" Here's the answer:

> 1Pet 5:10 *But the God of all grace, who has called you to His eternal glory in Christ, will, after you have suffered awhile, Him self equip, stabilize, strengthen, and firmly establish you.*

'nuf said.

Chapter Sixteen—

Technical School

Isn't it amazing how the principles we learn for leading our earthly physical life are also so appropriate for developing our spiritual life? No pain, no gain. Train, train, train.

Preparation is the key to successfully meeting any endeavor. The Training Instructor (T.I.), similar to God, has to test us. This testing is beneficial to us, personally. It not only lets the T.I. know how we're progressing, but it also lets us know what our body and mind can and can't [yet] accomplish. What it needs to be able to accomplish, and what areas we're going to have to work harder to make the grade. Similar to weight training, this progressive loading of our faith will yield greater results in the future.

For example, do you think Moses could have parted the Red Sea on his first trip to the beach? I don't think so. He had to first realize God's working within him, prior to accomplishing such spectacular feats.

God used Moses to accomplish many feats of power. But He also tested his physical and mental endurance. The peer pressure on Moses must have been incredible. Picture this, one million Israelis, bound in Egyptian slavery for more than 400 years. Helpless to save themselves. Suffering bitterly beneath burdens inflicted on them by their idol-worshipping masters. And now, having recently attained their freedom from bondage (Moses was educated on using his mouth for this to happen), they had to wander around [and around] in the desert for 40 "whining" years. Think of all the "cheese" the Israelis must have gone through.

If we think we've got it tough. Let's compare our difficulty with another aspect of Moses' life. After all, he didn't have the opportunity to gain a first class education, to go through a metered, disciplined, schooling process (Basic Training, Technical School, etc).

Moses had a really tough start in life. How many of you started right off the bat as he did? A true basket case. Usually, it takes most of us several years to fall into that trough. But Moses was accelerated down to this position within the first 3 weeks of his life. Whew! As a leader of men and nations, and a direct representative from God, he certainly had a steep learning curve to overcome.

> Deut 12:7 *Ye shall not do here this day, every man whatsoever is right in his own eyes.*

Say what? Let's translate this into the vernacular to describe what is NOT supposed to happen:

"I'm OK, you're OK."

"Do your own thing as long as it doesn't hurt anyone else."

This PC'ness just doesn't hack it. It's a crock and we all know it. How can we effectively combat the enemy if we're running around willy-nilly, doing our own thing, without a synchronized, planned, choreographed Ops Plan?

Again, we need to hark back to what we learned in Basic Training: TEAM effort.

What are WE doing with our talent(s)?

What we want or what God wants?

What are WE doing with our time? What we think is Ops effective or what God wants?

These are the kinds of questions that the Israelis neglected to ask during their forty year stroll in the wilderness. They were walking around (literally around, and around, and around) the physical [and spiritual] wilderness, saying politically correct stuff like, "I'm OK, you're OK". Operating within their [man-made] societal norms. Every person did what was right in his own eyes. There wasn't any prevalent sense of God as a sovereign king; the ultimate, all-powerful authority; absolute ruler of all the heavens and earth. Whassup with this picture?

God must have really gotten tired of this lameness: people acting like vagabonds, just tooling around the wilderness, waiting in disgust for them to implement the gifts he bestowed upon them. But, they just didn't have enough gumption or vision to grab the ball and run, to enter into Canaan. Canaan, the land of milk and honey. Crisp, clear water; green, grassy fields; fruits and vegetables ripe, waiting for harvest. Instead, the Israelis contented themselves by whining [no cheese!] about the manna, unwilling to look to Him to change their environment. Not willing to look to Him to supply them with strength, armor and weaponry.

Let's ask these same questions one more time in a personal manner:

What are YOU doing with your talents? What you want or what God wants?

What are YOU doing with your time? What you think is right or what God wants? Do you believe

God is in ultimate control? Do you believe God has the big picture, the CTP?

If so, then let's refocus the direction of these questions because you have already empowered Him to provide your SA. Correct?

What are you doing with the talents God has given you? What are you doing with God's time?

We know we don't really own or possess anything (talents, time, etc). All that we have are all given to us from God. We're just fortunate enough that He gave them to us. When a warfighter signs up with Jesus, he has just given Him all the rights, privileges, and royalties to re-establish the sovereignty of Him within his soul. The warfighter no longer needs to depend on his own soda-straw, myopic perception. He is now part of a team, a team driven by the CTP, the big picture, dedicated to accomplishing a far greater good than any human can foresee.

Technical School will reinforce concepts learned in Basic Training. It melds these concepts into functional applications and combat scenarios, while providing specialized skills to the warfighter. Tech School presents another level for integrating multi-source information inputs to the warfighter to use in combat operations. Knowing these things about you, His warfighter, God illustrates His presence as we progress through Tech School.

Isaiah 43:2 *When you pass through the waters*

This is an entry level difficulty. The swimming pool course prepares us for combat in still water; mud; and knee deep rice patties. The inherent dangers are stumbling, tripping, wet equipment, poisonous snakes and bugs.

I will be with you,
Reassurance from the CINC.

and when [you go] *through the rivers,*
This raises the level of difficulty bar up a notch. The water is moving: it has velocity, power. There are now additional dangers: drowning, loss of life and loss of equipment.

they shall not overwhelm you;
Jehovah Jireh. He will provide us with all our weapons, ESM, logistics and needs.

when you go through fire
This steps up the challenge even more than the previous ones. Protective gear is now required. Agility in flexing to various operational conditions is essential. Additional dangers include: fear, immobility, stressing out, severe wounds and pain.

you shall not be scorched;
Safety provided. No distractions will beset you.

or through flames,
This could be the highest challenge (the flames of hell?). Mental and physical agility are mandated. Absolute focus is required to successfully and safely complete the mission. Obvious dangers include but are not limited to: fuel on water; engulfed, encircled by flash fires. High stress, Ops Tempo max'ed out. Can't do it by ourselves. Gotta rely on the team. Leave it at the cross.

you shall not be burned.

100%. Success is the only choice we should consider. He's talking about us, all combative warfighters, fighting the fight, walking the walk, and on patrol in The Valley of Shadows and Death.

Whether you're on a surface vessel or in a rubber dinghy "going under" with your barrel plugged, or running through a blaze of [small arms and mortar] fire. He is with you. His purpose for your being at your present location will be completed. I, the Lord, am with you. Jesus has chosen [specifically] you, to accomplish [specifically] a mission. Focus your eyes on Him, and He will [safely and successfully] lead you through.

How many times as a student or while you were in training did you have the President, CEO or Head Shed, come to your classroom and give you the lesson? How many times, if ever, would one of these guys take the time to even write part of the training curriculum? Our Commander has taken the time to write the Ops Manual and the corresponding lesson plans for each of us. Check out Revelations 2 and 3. John is transcribing from His notes to write a letter to the seven churches. Each of these letters finishes with:

> *"He who is able to hear; let those who can hear; let everyone who can hear, listen...."*

See to it that you do not refuse Him who is speaking (i.e. if you can hear, you better listen).

> *For if they did not escape when they refused him who warned them on earth, [how] much less shall we escape if we reject him who warns from heaven.* Heb12:25

You might think a military tribunal convened for a court martial is serious business. Reread the last part of this verse. Jesus is in heaven now. He's the Commander. If you don't listen to what the Commander directs you to do, guess what! You won't hear Jesus saying, "Hasta la vista, baby" but rather… "I'll be back!" aka the Terminator.

Chapter Seventeen—

Learning and Understanding

Learning and understanding seem to fall hand in hand with each other. These two words are also frequently viewed as synonyms. But, guess what. They're not. These two words are as similar as ice cream, as Chocolate Chip is to Rocky Road. But they are fundamentally different in functionality, application, and taste.

So what is learning, and how do we learn effectively? Learning can be defined in several ways. To keep our focus on a warfighter's perspective, let's define "learning" in digital combat terminology: to implant an experience for immediate retrieval for later action.

People employ different means, methods, and mechanisms to enhance their learning capabilities. The Bible also differentiates between these various learning mechanisms. For instance, John describes a progressive learning pattern in I John 1:1-2

> First, "*They heard*,
> Then they *saw*,
> Next, they *touched the Word of Life* (Jesus);
> *then they testified to it and*
> then finally/consequently *proclaimed that Word.*"

Here the people used their sound, sight and touch receptors to enhance their database, verbalized the inputs received and then acted upon the inputs. God is always communicating. He uses these same procedures for the Holy Spirit to communicate with us today. We can hear Him, aurally and mentally. We can see Him by the mental images, visions and dreams He provides. We can still touch (literally) and feel (sensory) His (spoken and written) Word.

The next two steps, however, determine the rank and file among warfighters. These took action and proclaimed His Truth. Proclaim means to publicly announce or broadcast. This action will result in consequences. It will provide you with immediate feedback and put yourself out in front based on your faithfulness to Him. These actions are accomplished by His true prophetic and apostolic warfighters today.

Scientists, psychologists, and educators like to pontificate about the use of sensory perception as a key element in the learning process, as if they should be accredited with this "recent" discovery. As we see from the text above, this learning principle practiced by Jesus thousands of years ago is actually older than the hills. Or at least older than the written text in the Bible. Hmm-m-m. Scientists, psychologists, educators! Take a back seat. You're still just beginning to learn.

Now that we have "discovered" that learning can be acknowledged, implanted, absorbed, and archived from our different sensory receptors into our main database, how do we effectively learn what we just learned? (Eh??) Or, how do we prepare ourselves to put into action what we just learned?

For those of you forced into slave labor, at a young age, on a piano bench, you heard "practice, practice, practice" at least ten times a day. However, learning is more than just practice. Practice is going through the motor functions to accomplish an act. Doing it over and over again, until a groove, a rut is worn or formed. Practice ensures consistency in movement. There's a [big] technical difference between movement and action. Action implies a planned movement, but with room to flex, modify, and manipulate as changes are encountered in the operational environment.

Learning entails putting these actions into operations for testing, assessment, evaluation, and then further refinement. Learning is not static. It is not a constant. Learning is a dynamic animal. Changing, growing, hungry to hunt, to meet the foe toe-to-toe, and to conquer.

Learning requires us to experiment, to take risks, to challenge what we already know in order to embrace something entirely new. It means going beyond what we have been conditioned to see, hear, and understand (Matt 13:13). That's the dynamism of learning.

If learning is the Chocolate Chip, understanding is the Rocky Road in ice cream terminology. Proverbs 4:7 aptly states:

Though it cost you all you have, get understanding.

To understand a concept, a principle, and/or the functionality of an object, means "to put it together mentally [piece by piece], to comprehend [all the "ins and outs"], and then act" [to carry out, to execute, your newfound information].

Understanding is the consummate form of learning. The sensory receptors have already been energized, the inputs put into the database, and the full process of the learned element has been absorbed, verbalized, and acted upon. Assessment, evaluation and refinement of action has taken place, and further "process tuning" is occurring. The mental, emotional, physical, and spiritual number crunching, the association and differentiation between seemingly similar data elements and the cross-correlation of these effects and impacts, this is what entails the beginning of the understanding process. This is what it means to understand. This is what He wants us to be able to do.

He has laid the foundation for us to learn His TTPs, His ROE. The Holy Spirit is already in us. Empower Him through faith for reaching out to new understandings. Let Him take control. Understand His desires, yearnings, and direction. It is up to us to want to learn, and then to understand how to best employ it. Effectively knocking the socks off Satan and his troops!

As you can readily perceive, there will be [many] times when the Holy Spirit requires one to step out on faith, not by vision. This principle is even practiced today by coaches who want their players to excel. They ensure the athlete is capable of seeing victory even before it is seen with their eyes. Do athletes really win the race before they ever set foot on the track, or is it only upon breaking the tape? Are battles really won prior to the engagement, or only after the Bomb Damage Assessment is completed?

People like Albert Einstein, Henry Ford, etc. are said to be wise people. They were acclaimed to have wisdom. Why? Because they listened, watched, and acted upon their understanding. They were able to break out of their comfort zone. Their belief in their understanding happened first.

Gideon was also a great warrior. He and his 300 armed vagabonds conquered a massive enemy. Afterall, they were armed with trumpets and clay pots. Not a sword among them. Think about that.

The win occurs first in the mind, prior to the actual physical accomplishment. That is where action is pertinent. Pertinent? No way! That's where action is mandatory. God says it. Now, you! That's right, <u>you</u> sitting on your butt reading this. Get up and do it. **Now!**

Chapter Eighteen—

Intelligent Preparation for the Battlefield (IPB)

> 1Pet1:13a *Brace up your minds for action, therefore, and be alert,...*
>
> Habakkuk 2:1 *I will take my stand on my post, station myself on the tower, and watch to see what He will say to me; what answer I shall receive concerning my complaint. [2] The Lord answered me and said: "Write the vision!*

Vision = Having the plan and authority for executing His instructions, commands, and orders!

> *Make it plain upon tablets, so he who runs by may read it! [3] However, the vision waits for its appointed time; it hastens toward the end; it will not lie. If it lingers, wait for it; for it will certainly come; it will not lag.*

Battle managers, controllers, shooters, and support personnel normally want to operate on higher ground to observe the battle arena, to enhance their situational awareness, to watch and wait, to properly execute a plan.

Habakkuk portrays the modern day warfighter. He's standing guard, waiting and watching the battle arena. Waiting for more information; additional instructions; an answer to resolve his concerns. Ready to execute based on the information and current capabilities he possesses.

The Lord says, the answer is on its way. It will arrive at its appointed time. If it doesn't come immediately; don't sweat it. It is coming. Wait for it. The answer will not be deceitful, nor will it loiter aimlessly.

Have you ever been working in the yard or in the garage? You're nasty filthy, dripping sweat like a wet dog. But you're hungry. So you ask your youngest who is outside playing to have Mom fix a PB&J and coke. Your child lights off ready to execute your command. Proud as punch to help out.

Forty-five minutes later, you hose yourself off and go inside to reconnoiter the suspected transgressions. Here's what actually transpired after your request:

> After petting the pooch and playing with the cat, your child asked, "Mom, can you fix a PB&J and coke?" [So far, so good, right? A direct quote from your mouth.] Mom said, "Yes, but only after you put your toys back and get washed up."

You come into the house and there on the table is ½ of a PB&J with a short, warm "sippy" cup of coke. Your request was executed by your child. However, the intent for your instructions was garbled. Your child obeyed your command, explicitly. Timing and sense of urgency were expressed but the intent was misunderstood, and therefore, the outcome was put in a hovering "wait & hold" pattern.

Only via preparation [training and instruction] will we be able to hear or see the answer when it arrives. Does this make more sense now? As a warfighter we have to know how to express ourselves and how to keep looking for the answer. Without the proper preparation, instruction, and training, completing God's desires to the fullest just won't happen. We'll still be stumbling around the garage, malnourished, famished, and even the dog won't come near us. Eh?

> Psalms 32:8 *I will instruct you and teach you in the way you should go; I will counsel you and watch over you!* [9] *Do not be like the horse or the mule, which have no understanding but must be controlled by bit and bridle or they will not come to you.* [10] *Many are the woes of the wicked, but the Lord's unfailing love surrounds the man who trusts in Him!*

So much power in so few words! Another sign of a great leader, aye? Let's take these three statements apart for refinement to understand the inherent, organic principles herein:

> Verse 8a: *I will instruct you and teach you in the way you should go;*

Think of your new priority list regarding your life with Jesus. Do you just jump in and start doing?

Well the first question is "Doing what?" Generally speaking, your new priority list just doesn't undergo execution without understanding the tasks associated with it. I'm sure there are exceptions, but overall I'm fairly confident that incremental change is the "norm". Think of this process as learning a completely new skill, or wanting to play a new musical instrument. Don't let this be a daunting obstacle to you. Especially, if you're like me. I can play the radio and carry a tune in a five gallon bucket, but don't ask for a rhythmic swing while I'm lugging the bucket along. Ok?

Jesus says we need an instructor and a teacher. Man, are we lucky. I've met some instructors that shouldn't have ever been certified, and some teachers that couldn't teach their way out of a broken, "swinging on one hinge" screen door. But, we are specifically assigned to the Master of Education. He wrote each of our personal requirements according to our needs to execute His mission.

To acquire, grow and enhance any new skill, what does it take? Practice, motivation, dedication, sincerity, feedback, and more continuous practice to learn and understand. Feedback from our leaders and mentors is necessary to hone our strengths, to strengthen our weaknesses, and to ensure timeliness in team actions and responses.

Understanding comes from knowing your own weaknesses and strengths as well as the theoretical and application functionalities for attaining a professionalism in your new skill/priority assessment. "Wow! I never knew it was so complex!" I thought I just accepted Jesus into my heart and Bango-Pango, I received eternal life. Yes, that is true.

Look at the rest of the verse.

[8b]: *I will counsel you and watch over you!* If you listen to what the Master says, you will have the best counsel ever provided. Furthermore, those desiring to be true warfighters for Jesus will also be provided a personal watch (guardian, team leader, protector, bodyguard and more importantly your own personal spiritguard!).

Check out the next verse.

> [9]: *Do not be like the horse or the mule, which have no understanding but must be controlled by bit and bridle or they will not come to you.*

Now my Dad is an old farm boy. Spent most of his dear life behind two mules growing corn and tobacco. (True pronunciation is: 'BACca.) Both my Gran'pa and my Dad state that a mule is much smarter than a horse. By mentioning the horse first (the dumber of the two beasts), I think Jesus was trying to give us an optimistic lift in approaching Him.

An animated paraphrase could be similar to: "Don't be like the horse, who is likely to run at full throttle (without any vector or directional purpose).

Shoot, even a mule can more effectively expend his energy. The only problem here is the inherent motivation factor, i.e. stubborn hard-headedness. I'm your instructor, your teacher, your counselor. Have faith in me. Listen and heed. When I provide you with instruction, accomplish it as I have indicated. Do not be one to hear, nod your head like a dog in the back window of a car, and not act [on your own volition]. Be a warfighter! If I wanted a response similar to a horse, I would call on it and not on you."

> 2Pet 1:3 *For His divine power has bestowed on us every requisite for life and godliness, through knowing Him who called us to His own glory and excellence.. Instructions for knowing our gift and what we're supposed to do. [10] Exert yourselves the more then, brothers, to confirm [validate your faith by what you do] your calling and election, for if*

you practice these things you will never stumble.

If you're musically "declined" as I am, but wanted to master the playing of a musical instrument, what would be the first fundamental step toward accomplishing this? The first step would probably be to rent an instrument, hire an instructor/tutor and practice until you "...*know... what you're supposed to do.*"

Now if you only spend 1 hour a week with your instrument, how proficient will you become? If you only spend 1 hour a week searching to know your God-given gift, to validate your faith, to confirm your calling, how long will it take? What level of "expertise" will you really ever attain?

In order to execute His plan, we must first intelligently prepare ourselves for receiving His instructions. We've gone through the training. Now we need to apply what we've learned. We need to understand the functional applications and "Watch" for His timing to execute His order!

The Armory

Chapter Nineteen—

"Armor !!!"

It's Purpose. The inception for using armor was to protect the warfighter from offensive, attacking forces. However, after the course of a couple vigorous battles, innovative warfighters discovered practical operational utility and developed expertise in using defensive entities (i.e. armor) in an offensive capacity. Hence, the derivation of the phrase, "The best defense is a good offense."

The concept of using armor is well noted throughout man's history and in the Bible. As a matter of fact, it is a direct order from God to use His armor effectively. God himself is a very tactical God. He supplies us with just the correct equipment and communication links required to get His purpose accomplished. However, God's armor isn't for defending His fortress, but for executing His commands (offensive operations) out in the combat zone.

The forces of Satan (OPFOR) are certainly offensive (both in the figurative and literal sense). Therefore, we need to ensure we use His armor effectively. The enemy will be fearful of our confidence. They cannot discourage us or distract us from our spiritual tasking.

It's Use

> *For though we live in the world we do not wage war as the world does. The weapons we fight with are not the*

weapons of the world. On the contrary, they have divine power to demolish strongholds. 2Cor 10:3-4

Unbeknownst to many earthly warfighters, man uses the same God-given commands and warfighting principles to engage in combat with other men today. As surprising as that may sound, it is correct. Earthly combat Tactics, Techniques, and Procedures and Principles of Warfare have their origin from The Holy Bible. They are historically derived directly from God's SPINS (Special Instructions).

Christian warfighters are always called to be on their guard (1Thes 5:6, 1Peter 5:8, 9). By declaring war against Satan, and his evil spirits and demons, a warfighter's situational awareness must remain at the highest heightened state of awareness, recognition and readiness. For whenever we praise the name of Jesus and reach out for His power, whenever we call out for "reinforcements" and understanding, Satan's kingdom of darkness undergoes bombardment by [divine] PGMs (Precision Guided Munitions). This really torques him off! He hates all friends of Jesus.

Jesus' warfighters are especially on the top of Satan's list because of their constant effective, synchronized offensive assaults on his kingdom of darkness. We all know Satan lost at the cross. Satan hates admitting his second fiddle status; his unbullet-proof rogue Colonel status. Tough nuts, loser. We're going to scrub more rock salt in that wound. Hooah!

God is an experienced, innovative, warfighting operator. As such, He issues us armor that can be used for both defensive and offensive operations. God addresses a defensive posture in Jeremiah 1:18

See!
Hey! Look at me when I'm talking to you. This is the Lord speaking!

(Please take note that in Biblical times, they didn't have the word "Hey." Their speech followed more along the lines of what my grandma would say to me... "Now see here!" as she was trying to wrench grandpa's corn pipe out of my hand.)

Not an implied threat, but certainly worthy of taking note for impending actions that could follow if one didn't perk their ears up and listen.

I, on My part,
because I choose to do this, to test your true-standing with me; to test your mettle; to progress you in accomplishing great things during your earth-bound life

have made you today as a beleaguered city

You are under attack right now, even if you don't realize it. The enemy is camped outside, conducting probes, instigating skirmishes, and preparing for a full-out assault.

as an impregnable fortress, and as an unassailable stronghold against the entire land...

God is not portraying a foxhole or a bunker to hunker down in, but a fortress; completely self-contained and lacking no resources; complete with high-tech (sci-fi) armaments, an Integrated Air Defense System, an unbelievable Ground Attack Force, water, real food (not boil and shake stuff) etc. Hang tough. Jesus has your "6" covered. Actually, he has your "3", "6", "9" and "12" covered, in 3-D. Whoa! Think about that. His is the complete, comprehensive, and still tactically useful picture. Tap into it.

God ensures our success in offensive actions to include attack operations. Before reading the following, familiarize yourself with reading and understanding the Op Order. Be attentive to punctuation! Capital/upper case "H" (e.g. He) designates our Commander-In-Chief, Jesus. Lowercase letter "h" (e.g. he) designates the OPFOR leader, Satan. Let's proceed:

> 1John 4:4 *Greater is He* (our CINC) *that is in you than he* (OPFOR) *that is in the world!*

God's detailed Battle Plan (Executive Order #0000001) was to allow Jesus to be shamefully and inhumanely executed by people who were directly influenced by the OPFOR. And then, once Satan's troops were rejoicing, and celebrating their perceived "victory," Jesus shocked their socks off by conquering death and thereby, being able to re-engage them in combat.

Think about it. The OPFOR thought because Jesus was in a human form (a weak shell of a mortal body) that if the body died, it would trap Jesus' being/Spirit in it also. Wrong-o moose-breath! He arose. He is alive! Prepare to meet your prescribed termination point, buck-o!

God-supplied armor comes in many forms and fashions. His armor possesses multi-faceted functionalities. However, this section is going to just briefly discuss six major spiritual armored components that He specifically addresses, their historical derivation, and then correlate God's and man's functional application for each component.

These components are:

1. The Sword
2. The Shield
3. The Helmet
4. The Breastplate
5. The Belt
6. The Shoe

His armor is intended for those physically and mentally prepared to wear it and to use it properly, and effectively. His armor is not issued to us to hide behind. It is issued to enable the warfighter to become more effective in engaging the enemy. It is issued to enable the warfighter to become more confident and aggressive in successfully going toe-to-toe with the OPFOR (Satan's troops). Armor is made for warfighters, not for skulking wimps. God supplies us with multi-purposed armor and weaponry. Use it, lose it, or give it to someone who needs it!

Chapter Twenty—

The Sword of the Spirit

Introduction. A sword most frequently is considered a weapon rather than a piece of armor. However, like armor, it can defend the warfighter from an attacker, as well as protect the "user/holder" during offensive maneuvers.
The sword is the first piece of gear issued to a warfighter. Without it, a "warfighter" is technically (and realistically) a prime target of opportunity for the OPFOR. Armor not properly issued, worn, or used can actually be a detriment when [attempting] to engage the enemy. The OPFOR readily recognizes this and will enthusiastically seek to exploit, reveal, and attack any new found weakness. God wants us to use each and every piece of His armor in an effective manner. Therefore, the Sword is included in His TO&E.

Historical Perspective. Most of us are familiar with several kinds of swords. The Broadsword used by the Norsemen, Vikings, and Conan is one such example. The broadsword is a long, heavy sword that demands great physical strength and power to effectively employ it. In such a person's hands, the broadsword is capable of slicing through large trees in one fell swoop.
 The immediate image of a broadsword conjures up a picture of a heavy, simple blade, with an intricately carved and molded hand-piece. The Broadsword was worthy enough to be passed

down from generation to generation. Its main purpose was to protect its bearer in combat. Otherwise, it remained proudly displayed in a prominent location, such as over a stone fireplace, for all to observe.

The Samurai Sword is another sword that is readily recognized. It too is an object of awe, desire, and pride. Handcrafted by only the best artisans for elite families. It was also passed down from generation to generation. The sword itself is not only a fine piece of classic art in steelsmithing, but even its cover and holding rack were exclusively crafted for each individual exquisite sword.

The Samurai Sword demands a mental image of a bright, flashing sword, with an extremely sharp and piercingly hard edge. Its weight and balance enable the swordsman to use it in performing astonishingly swift aerial gymnastics.

The Samurai Sword was generally used for combat, but could also be used for festivities and to show one's physical prowess and demeanor.

A more current sword that garners immediate recognition is the sword used by the US Marine Corps (USMC). This sword is also a highly prized item. It automatically evokes emotions of pride, loyalty, devotion [at all cost] and pure strength. Its simplicity and light-weight give the swordsman a high degree of dexterity in controlling its execution. This sword is used for formal occasions and to reinforce the traditional principles of the USMC. Semper Fi!

As indicated above, swords are ardently, venerated objects. You can tell a lot about a person who owns a sword. There is a common intertwining thread among those that possess one. Owning a sword symbolizes a passion or desire for history and tradition, and brings about many deep, heart-felt emotions.

The sword is usually formally displayed in a location that brings awe to anyone that takes in its sight. A magnificent object, it deserves to be treated as a respected and yet, a dangerous object. Although the sword hasn't played a significant part in recent wars or battles due to technological advances in munitions and modern weaponry, it's effective employment and function as an issued piece of armor [and weaponry] is still representative in today's battles.

For example, effective employment demands frequent study, practice, and action. Without mastering and maintaining familiarity with the "action" of the sword, it either becomes relegated as only an object that hangs on a wall, or an object capable of endangering the user's life.

This is especially true when grabbing the handle of the greatest sword of all: The Sword of The Lord --- His Word, a venerated and hallowed piece of armor and weaponry. His Sword is sharper than any two-edged sword ever made (Heb 4:12). It is harder than any diamond; swifter than any electron; capable of dispensing justice and discipline; providing guidance, direction and Truth to all that listen and desire to understand.

His Sword is multi-faceted. It is portrayed in many different venues. It can be displayed in hardcopy, i.e. the Holy Bible. In times gone bye, the family Bible was displayed as an object of respect and joy. Fortunately, there are still families that maintain this respected tradition. God's Sword can also be revealed in His voice by issuing a word of wisdom or knowledge at the right moment. Allow me to share this one incredible moment with you as an example:

I was reading Derek Princes book, "*They Shall Expel Demons*" and was evaluating the bouts of depression he was encountering. This was pertinent to me, because just a few weeks prior to reading his book, I was suffering real wall-banging headaches whenever I attempted to work on this book. I was also going through a phase of feeling fear, apprehension, and procrastination when reading anything related to Jesus. I realized this was a parallel experience to Derek's experience with depression. I immediately prayed Derek's written prayer to Jesus, to not allow Satan or his troops to hassle me, to make Himself known to them by His working in me.

BOOM! The fear, apprehension and headache ---- GONE!

Instantaneous! Just like it never existed!

God's Sword can also be revealed by a vision, shown to your mind's eye as happened to Daniel in interpreting King Nebuchadrezzar's dream (Daniel 2). However, allow me to provide another more current, personal example:

Last year, our lawn pump quit working. The motor should have been toast because it's only supposed to run a few minutes without water circulating through it. Needless to say, it ran for hours the day before we noticed it wasn't operating. I took a full day to replace parts and pieces, mixed with blood, sweat and knuckles. Absolutely nothing was working. My mental patience had already turned into mental "patients".

In a moment of human weakness and frailty, I looked up at His sky, it was a nice pale blue color. A cool breeze kicked up and I thought, "Why are we surprised by answered prayer?" This thought came out of nowhere. So I responded to it by offering a prayer to Him. I acknowledged that "it will only be by your grace, effort, and work Jesus that this thing operates."

Well, I chuckled to myself, at God taking the time to do something so miniscule. The lawn pump Ops Manual warns, "Do NOT run the pump for more than 7 minutes without water." Our personal system only requires three minutes to push out the first water (when it's working). Seven minutes had already clocked out, no cigar. I walked to the control switch, with my hand on the OFF switch and said, "Well Lord, just in case, here's one last look for you." Peeked around the corner and ..."Why are we surprised by answered prayer?" Whew! He is a wild, crazy, and ALIVE!!! Master.

Under coercion a sword can evoke the truth from its respondent. The Sword of the Lord, His Word, is TRUTH. No contentions, no coercion, ... fact.

Like the swords made by man, His Sword needs to be formally displayed for all. His display case is our life. We need to re-present Him in our daily lives' actions.

His Sword is a venerated, righteous entity, worthy of being brought to everyone's immediate attention, to be looked upon as holy, good, and correct. His (capital H "His") Sword needs to be treated in exactly the same manner as a man-made sword. It mandates one to continually study, practice (belief + action), listen, learn and understand. Without these, His Sword [likewise] becomes nothing more than an object of curiosity, or even worse, an object capable of misuse and abuse, causing harm, and capable of endangering both the holder and the recipient, eternally.

Give me power Lord, to swing the Sword of your Word with strength and accuracy; to slice through all temptations, Satanic troops, and to successfully conquer according to Your Ops Plan. Give me the strength to turn spiritual plowshares into Swords (capital "S").

Chapter Twenty One—

The Shield of Faith

Historical Perspective. The shield was the first piece of armor available to warfighters. Initially, it was employed as a defensive piece of gear. However, warfighting "operators" soon found interesting methods to also use it in an offensive mode, to attack the enemy.

When one thinks of a shield, it invokes a vision of a Roman soldier or gladiator using a large frontal, flat plate for protection. The shield was originally intended to protect its user during a frontal engagement. Soldiers later effectively employed it to shield their flanks and heads as they were moving forward, toward a target.

Function. You'll notice the word "shield" is defined as a verb. (A verb is an action word for those of you who have been away from school for too long). As such, it portrays a vigorous activity, an entity with inherent motion. As an entity it is an object (noun), but an object with merit and utility. It represents an object in an active, engaging environment. Stillness, lack of activity, immobility (couch-veggie) is definitely not a part of His plan for the Shield.

If God wanted His Shield to portray an immobile state, I'm confident, He would have used the word "Cone" instead of "Shield" (i.e. "Cone of Faith" rather than "Shield of Faith"). A cone depicts an inactive, non-committal, somewhat stationary, geometrically shaped object. It is adverse to forward action. It is not conducive to mobility. Lying on its side, it will roll, but only as a puppy chases its tail (round and round and...). Put it on its point, and "splat", it will be back in the "puppy" mode again. Put its widest end down (ice cream in the dirt) and it's fairly stationary and somewhat stable.

The cone actually does offer a [temporarily] protected, comfort zone for those who [whiningly] hope for no confrontations or encounters by friend or foe, i.e. for those comfy couch potatoes or wannabe warfighters. But, it is certainly susceptible to penetration and dislodgment. With a concerted effort by a few, the cone is easily upset and disposed to lie on its side, again. In this orientation, it offers no protection and no avenue of escape to those who ignorantly remain within.

But God didn't use the word "cone". He used the word "shield". In contrast, a shield is a very flexible armored piece of equipment. At the warfighter's determination, it can be whipped in front to provide protection for a given time, or it can be held off to the side still enabling protection, but also assisting in offensive actions.

Action, that is the key word. The Shield of the Lord is used in an action-based, present tense form. It is meant to be used in both defensive and offensive [armored] operations.

A larger concept of a shield is the fortress. A fortress in the human concept of operations (CONOP) is a mighty, heavily reinforced, permanently located structure. It is not mobile. It is not transportable. It is a solid structure that is not moving. That is its primary strength.

God's fortress is stronger than any structure a human could possibly desire to build. But, unlike any humanly built fortress, God's fortress is also tactically oriented and it is mobile. Yes, it is deployable. It can move along with the warfighter, providing an all-encompassing armored shield for 3D-360° protection. It is a most formidable entity to the OPFOR. God's fortress provides us with a safe haven, a retreat, a place to regroup and re-energize. It is okay to use it as this, for so it was intended.

In fact, David claims this condition, this promise that God made to his warfighters in Psalms 144:2 :

> " ...my Fortress, ...my Shield in whom I have taken refuge."

BUT, it is critical to recognize that a refuge, a safe haven, a retreat is only intended to provide temporary shelter, temporary shielding, during the worst part of a storm, a tornado, a battle, etc. It is only used until the worst conditions are over and passed by. It is not used to establish a new permanent residence.

Similarly, His Fortress provides the warfighter with a Shield during the worst part of a battle. However, it is supposed to be used only as a temporary respite from danger. An appropriate example would be when we are forced to dive into a bunker during an artillery or mortar barrage. We're safe inside, taking cover during the action, then immediately back into position pushing out hot lead when the barrage subsides.

God commands us to use His Fortress exactly in this manner. We need to use it [only] as a temporary defensive retreat when the forces of evil (OPFOR) have caught us off-guard and pounded on us a bit too much. We don't take up permanent residence there; we don't allow it to become our new comfort zone box. We emerge from it ready to face the next battle, ready for the next test. We whip our Sword back out in front of our Shield, ready to re-initiate the attack, now as more experienced, smarter warfighters. We're now more capable of using His Fortress as a Shield, as a battering ram to knock down, destroy, decimate any forces of evil that dare stand in the way, or even in the proximity of the path we're travelling in His footsteps.

God demands that we remain tactically mobile. His mandate: Faith requires action. This is the basis for the US Army's mandate: A moving target is harder to hit.

> *"I put all my trust in you Jesus and I know this Shield of my faith will protect me from all that Satan will throw at me. Increase my faith* [my ACTION]. *You are my God. My times are in your hands."* Pastor Pa^{t}ul.

Chapter Twenty Two—

The Helmet of Salvation

Historical Perspective. The helmet was the first piece of armor requiring the services from a specialist to hand form its fit to each warfighter's head. Early helmets were made from the hides of animals (just like the leather helmets used by football players in the hey days after WWII). The helmet quickly evolved from solely providing an operational "safety" requirement to an entity that made a fashion statement among warfighters and warfighting wannabes. Pretty feathers, plumes, jewels, and shiny metallic straps, spikes, and decorative devices attached to the helmet soon came into vogue. Artisans and skilled craftsman were then conscripted into service to work for the governor's wife's cousin in his shop: Harry's Helmets. Harry had a real quippish logo. I forget what it actually said, but that is immaterial at this point.

Function. The helmet is an integral part of armor issued to the warfighter. The basic design and functional application of a helmet enables the warfighter to fight through critical situations, to quickly recover from blows to the head or an otherwise deadly assault. It provides physical protection to the warfighter's head and mental faculties. It enables the warfighter to overlook, to not even be hindered by, or be cognizant of the occasional clanging, banging, and face-to-face head-butting with the OPFOR. It provides the protection that makes these events [at most] just mere annoyances. Following His direct command in

> 1Pet1:13a *Brace up your minds for action,*

This is a direct command from God that enlists both a physical and mental requirement on the warfighter. The physical requirement mandates the use of strapping on a helmet. Heightened Situational Awareness and preparing for an impending, vigorously tough encounter with the OPFOR more than establish the mental requirement.

> *therefore, and be alert*

Wearing the helmet [armor] keeps our minds in tune and focused for what we are doing…. His will; His purpose; focus, Focus, FOCUS!

God issues warfighters His helmet of protection. The helmet enables the warfighter to keep [His] the Commanders' Priority Target List (PTL) in focus. A warfighter that keeps his eyes on Jesus is unstoppable. Straying off His path won't happen. Obstacles, booby-traps, and ambushes that Satan lays in the path are not encountered because the warfighter's eyes are only on Jesus.

Additionally, His helmet also acts as a hardened, anti-jam antenna. It's impervious to electromagnetic pulses (EMP) initiated by Satan to distract us. It enables us to more clearly receive His direction and guidance, eliminates signal modulation, and electromagnetic interference put out by foreign entities. Thereby keeping our eyes, ears, and mind's eye focused on His holy priorities.

> *And do not conform to the present world system, but be transformed by the renewal of your mind, so as to sense for yourselves what is the good and acceptable and perfect will of God.* Romans 12:2

Protect my head, Lord: my eyes that I may see, my ears that I may hear and listen, my mind that I may think and understand, and my mouth that I may speak the words You give me. Fill my mind, soul, and spirit with your power, joy, and truth.

Chapter Twenty Three—

The Breastplate of Righteousness

Introduction. The breastplate is fundamentally an up-close and personal "wrap-around" shield. Critical operation zones (heart and lungs) are heavily reinforced, while zones requiring more mobility are still provided protection, without sacrificing or restricting operational requirements (i.e. movement).

Historical Perspective. Physicians played an integral part in the design of this piece of armor. The original breastplates quickly developed from mere pieces of wood and hide attached by straps hanging from the shoulders to exquisite pieces of metal work.

Think back to the fine breastplate pieces the Roman soldiers and Caesar wore in Julius Caesar. You think Miss America has a hard time squeezing into her dresses after chowing down at a pork BBQ buffet? These guys really had it tough... metal doesn't stretch but compresses the skin. Oooh-ouch! After the Renaissance, breastplate armor fell out of favor with the local bureaucrats and historic warfighters returned to the basic slab-sided, cold-rolled [armor-plated] steel to protect themselves.

Function. One of the first most impressionable examples I remember was the one Clint Eastwood used in [which flick was it?] Fist Full of Dollars/Hang 'Em High/The Good, Bad & Ugly? I saw these three together so many times at the Drive-In, I can't discern which is which. But I do know Clint used it at about three hours and 17 minutes into the show. Trust me.

A more current example is depicted by today's foot soldier and SWAT member. What is one of the first pieces of armor put on their body? The [kevlar] breastplate. This breastplate protects the heart and vital organs to keep the warfighter strong, healthy, and mobile in a tactically challenging environment. It also provides the wearer with mental confidence in executing the assigned mission's requirements.

Similarly, His [spiritual] Breastplate of Righteousness also protects the heart and lungs. In addition, it protects the soul and spirit of the warfighter. With confidence that God is protecting your body and spirit, executing His commands and following His ROE is a natural function.

> *In righteousness you will be established: Tyranny will be far from you; you will have nothing to fear. Terror will be far removed; it will not come near you... No weapon formed against you will prevail,...* Isaiah 54:14, 17

With God's Breastplate of Righteousness secured about your body, the warfighter can be impervious to fear. Terror and tyranny are not even considered for the ensuing battle. The weapons of the OPFOR turn out to be mere annoyances, distractions at best. You're able to walk through the Valley of

Shadows and Death with complete confidence. Confident that whoever or whatever is stupid enough to confront you will meet a deliberate and terminating end.

Be Bold! Be Strong!
Good Hunting!

Chapter Twenty Four—

The Belt of Truth

Historical Perspective. The Belt was actually the first piece of armor requiring bureaucratic "coordination". [Note: "Coordination" is the first governmental oxymoron, also.] This is the first occurrence whereby the warfighter is introduced to multi-tasking.

Government officials acknowledge the inefficiency of the warfighter in only having two hands to hold one (1) each sword and one (1) each shield. However, the CEO of Samson's Scabbard Company was a very innovative and influential persona, aka, he personally knew (and sponsored) the governor and thereby "influenced" the creation of a belt to hold:

- one (1) each Samson Army Knife, guaranteed to whittle, stick, and flick with a nominal six (6) months Mean-Time-Between-Sharpening (MTBS). MTBS, the precursor to MTBF, see Acronym list, with
- one (1) each specially designed Sammy's Scabbard Cover,
- one (1) each water container (bringing long-range combat to the forefront), and
- one (1) each satchel to carry three (3) each dried fruit (apple or orange), two (2) ounces each dried meat (bovine or deer), and one (1) each deck of (49) cards.

Hence the expression "a few cards short of a full deck."

Function. The belt is a linchpin to our overall physical well-being. Think of it, literally. The belt:

-Keeps our pants up, our shirt tucked in.

-Keeps our ammo belt with all the accessory pouches in place.

-Provides a latching point for the canteen.

-Offers the suspenders a hook to hold various pieces of required equipment and

 protective gear.

-Provided one of the best lines in *The Karate Kid*, i.e. J.C. Penney.

-Offers the resource for cutting notches in, after successful combat operations.

His Belt keeps all aspects of our immediate life (both spiritually and physically) in an organized efficient state. It helps us keep our focus on His priorities. Literally, it keeps all of our stuff together. Without the Belt our actions and life would be in a constant state of disarray, always pulling up our pants, picking up dropped and banged up gear, getting distracted by the infinite, meaningless, miniscule items that occur each day, that seemingly keep us from maintaining any kind of forward progress. (Whew!)

The Truth is Jesus. He tells us who we are, and gives us direction to accomplish our true mission. With our eyes on Him, He gives us focus, our Prioritized Target List. As His appointed warfighters, our wearing the Belt of Truth properly directs our actions in accordance with His Rules of Engagement, Operation Orders, etc.

Chapter Twenty Five—

The Shoes of the Gospel of Peace

Historical Perspective. The last basic enhancement to the long-range combat warfighter. High top, low top, cleat and vibram soled; steel toe, box toe; lace, zip, tie; medium, narrow and wide. Need more be said? Shoes come in an unquantifiable assortment of form, fit, and function. A good shoe is as necessary as a good rifle. Just ask Imelda Marcos.

Are the shoes of peace represented by sandals, flip-flops or combat boots? Many people prefer to envision peace as Jimi Hendrix did with flowers, sandals, and the attitude that everything and everybody is just hunky-dory fine. Unfortunately, Satan makes a "peaceful coexistence" impossible. Good and evil just cannot get along together. Where there is [a perceived] peace[ful weakness], Satan will attempt to exploit it. He will attempt to twist it to his advantage, to gray the area between good and evil, and right and wrong. To make it OK not to make a decision, not to take a stand, to become immobile. (Target ahead!) Just ask any knowing descendant of Adam and Eve.

Unlike the significant input by physicians in developing the breastplate there is no known direct linkage between podiatrists and the governmental bureaucracy. It just happened. There were shoes to sell and the government bought them. There's water front property for sale in southern Arizona. That's their story, and they're sticking to it.

Function. So what role does "Gospel" have in this [podiatrist's] section of [Peaceful?] armor? When you think of the word, gospel, what image appears in your mind? Do you think of a gospel choir: singing and swaying, clapping their hands, shouting joy, praise and victory? Do you think of a minister, Bible in hand, telling the Truth like it is? Rightly so.

The word "gospel" evokes action. These Shoes of the Gospel of Peace are active participants in the peace process. They enable a peace to exist. [Note: I didn't say a peaceful, "Why can't we all just get along" coexistence, Rodney.] They enforce the Commander's Orders. They assist warfighters in their responsibilities to walk and run, to carry out His will for peace. Yes, these shoes are for restoring peace of mind and heart to all. Yes, these shoes will be used against those enemies of Jesus.

> *I have given you authority to trample on snakes and scorpions and to overcome all the power of the enemy* [i.e. kick some butt]; *nothing will harm you!* Luke 10:19

Be Bold! Be Strong! ACT! Proclaim the name of Jesus, the Prince of Peace, King of Kings, Lord of Lords, Jehovah Nissi the Conqueror! Claim His power. Disseminate the orders (Action). Disperse the enemy (Action). Hallelu-jah! Look out Satan, we're going to ruin your day (Result)!

Summary

Dress for success. Wear His armor as designed.
- Wear it properly for effective, successful combat operations.
- Wear it actively. Employ it. Don't hang it on the wall or use it to waltz down the "cat-walk" with your [Annie] Oakley shades on.
- Wear it to keep focus on His vision.
- Wear it and expect good hunting!

Battle Management

Chapter Twenty Six—

Battle Management BMC4I

John 10:11-18: *I am the good* [Supreme Commander] *shepherd;*
I know my [warfighters] *sheep and*
my [warfighters] *sheep know me---*
just as the Father knows me and I know the Father---and
I lay down my life [I took the bullet]
for [each warfighter] *the sheep.*
I have other [warfighters, some are trained, others are still in training] *sheep*
that are not of this [Joint Special Force] *sheep pen.*
I must bring them also. They too will listen to my voice, and
there shall be one [Force, one Command] *flock and one* [Supreme Commander] *shepherd.*
The reason my father loves me is that I lay down my life [I voluntarily took the bullet for each warfighter and physically died]*---*
only to take it up [beat death, and came back to life] *again.*
No one takes it from me, but I lay it down of my own accord. I have authority to lay it down and authority to
take it up again [I am the Ruler, even over life and death].
This command I received from my Father.

  The CINC/Supreme Commander gave His life for you. He willingly took the bullet and died. He stepped out in front of it, just for you, on His own accord. He laid His life down for you and then miraculously took it up again. This was all part of His plan. What are you willing to do in return for the One who did this for you?

Our earthly warfighting capability is comprised of three distinct but uniquely intertwined entities:
- Battle managers
- Command and Control elements, and
- Shooters

Our spiritual warfighting capability is comprised of three distinct but uniquely intertwined entities: (Was that an echo?)
- Jesus
- Pastor
- Servant

Is there a correlation between the hierarchical/organizational structure? Shoot yeah, there is. Is this coincidental? Determine for yourself. Let's look at these from, first, a hierarchical structure and then from an operational perspective to view any potential relationships.

BM stands for Battle Management or Battle Managers, not for what you hope your little tyke does after he eats to keep healthy, Ok?

These are the leaders of the war effort, the goal setters and grand strategizers. Starting off with the CINC and going down through the ranks to the operations strategists, planners, and execution authorities. These folks are generally not up front on the battle lines, but swamped in a crowded area lined with computers, electronic whiteboards, wires running in all crazy directions, and maps, acetate, and grease pencils everywhere. They are in charge of running the war effort. They're watching and observing how things progress. Quite simplistically, they are the audience to the actual trigger pulling, pickle-button pushing means of destruction.

God is certainly the CINC. King of kings. Lord of lords. The One and only.

Command and Control (C2) elements serve as the interface, the liaison between the BM and shooter. The C2 guys orchestrate and guide the shooter into position prior to the actual shot being taken.

The Pastoral element should be/oughta be your spiritual leader acting as a knowledgeable interface between your spiritual and earthly life. If not, its time to find a true experienced interface to assist you in blazing trails and praying for direction, guidance, intercession, and resolution.

The Shooter: Although all are part of the warfighting process, this is the participant we envision as the "true" [stereotypical] warfighter. The shooter. He who pulls the trigger. He who screams through the air riding rockets of flame, unleashing untold harm onto the enemy. Try and defeat this, bubba. Zoom, boom, pow. I'll be back home before Dan Rather talks to you tonight.

The servant: Hey! This could [should?] be you. One who carries out his leaders' orders, commands, requests, desires, does what is needed without being asked. Continuously strives to do better. Maintains focus on prioritized items and events. Able to discern when activities require action. Knows how to search out an answer. Tried, tested, and true. Executes the belief principle on a continual basis, e.g. faith, action.

Battle Management within the spiritual ops environment becomes a very complex task. After all,

> *we are not fighting against people made of flesh and blood, but against persons without bodies—the evil rulers of the unseen world, those mighty satanic beings and great evil princes of darkness who rule this world; and against huge numbers of wicked spirits in the spirit world.* Eph 6:12

This is war. We need shooters, whether it's ground-pounding riflemen (i.e. daily praying warfighters and workers) or fighter jocks (i.e. pastors, apostles, prophets, and evangelists). But we also need cops to **Watch!** (Mark 13:37). Intel to provide discernment (Jude 22, 23). Cooks to provide food to the masses (5 loaves/2 fishes, Matt. 14:19), as well as controllers, and battle managers. The above listed groups are part of the core people providing care and updating information to assist in winning the various multi-faceted aspects of this war.

Therefore, having a common purpose is mandatory: Jesus.

A common focus is necessary: Overcoming Satan.

To accomplish this, we can't judge or compare each other based on our own personal assignment or abilities. It takes a team effort to overcome an intelligent enemy. How much more of a synchronized team effort is mandated to overthrow the Master of Evil? The one who is expert for preying on our most subtle weaknesses. No task is too great, or too small for him to continue in his attempt to weaken our position with Jesus.

Chapter Twenty Seven—

Centralized Command - Decentralized Execution

Centralized Command and Decentralized Execution is a cornerstone for the way our military forces engage in combat. Centralized Command enables those in control (e.g. Commander in Chief, Joint Forces Commander, Joint Forces Air/Land Component Commander, etc.), or those who dictate the battle, to maintain a clearer picture of the overall battle or war.

Battle Managers are a key element in this structure. Their focus is on winning the battle or war. They operate on a very high level, away from the details and technical aspects that enable their strategies and orders to be implemented and executed. They [preferably] don't have the time or the expertise to get involved in low level decision-making, such as deciding the specific timing and route for servicing a target.

Note "service" is really a nice term for addressing destruction. But please be cognizant, destruction is not always the preferred action taken against a target. There are other options available that can be more efficient, cost effective and timely. For instance, targets can be exploited (kept out of harm's way to gain more information from the specific target), isolated (physically, electronically, or logistically cut off), damaged (temporarily put out of operation; maintenance actions required), or destroyed (to smithereens). These decisions are made from the centralized command level.

Decentralized Execution entails descending from the high level Battle Manager's perspective down into the weeds of Operations. Mingling with operators that know how each piece of equipment works; how it is best employed; determining specifically how to complete the assigned task. For example, if the Battle Managers direct a target to be destroyed, the order would be floated down to a level where it could be determined whether an air strike or ground assault was the best option to satisfy the order. If an air strike was the better option, then pilots and Intel would determine numerous variables and planning options regarding the flight route. Just a few of these elements would include: Which route to fly. When and where a high level or nap of the earth altitude profile would be used. How they would approach the target (airspeed, azimuth, etc.). Which aircraft would fly in first. What is the firing sequence of munitions. How they would depart the target area, etc. etc. etc.

Similar as Centralized Command, Jesus (the CINC) issues orders to engage a target in order to win the battle against Satan. He maintains a clear picture of the combat arena for us. He issues orders, provides guidance and direction for us to effectively accomplish His objectives: e.g. Destroy that target. Rescue that person. Defend that community. One of His most renowned orders is The Ten Commandments.

These commands(!) give us direction and goals to accomplish His mission. However, in order to execute those commands we have to go back down into the weeds of Operations. Down to the guys who determine Decentralized Execution.

We team with the Battle Managers (pastor, apostles, and prophets) for interpretation and recommendations to execute His orders. Operators (elders, team leaders, and fellow warfighters, etc.) choose their employment tactics. They determine how they are going to fight the battle, which defenses and offensive modes to employ, when to call in reinforcements (angels, the Holy Spirit, and/or Jesus Himself) for protection and to listen for further guidance as the war progresses.

Chapter Twenty Eight—

Rules Of Engagement

The Rules of Engagement (ROE) dictate the high level view for setting the laws that govern the conduct concerning combat operations. They stipulate under what circumstances a defensive posture must be maintained, as well as, when approval is given for commencing offensive operations, i.e. to become a shooter instead of a target.

In simplest laymen's terms, the ROE states "How" the game is played and when the "game" position changes its intensity to actual conflict. The goal for establishing these rules is to protect our team members until a satisfactory level of [current/temporary] peace is reached. These are the rules of man.

God has also provided us with Rules of Engagement. However, unlike man's rules, His ROE isn't situational dependent. It doesn't change with every variation in circumstance. It is consistent.

Our "game" as spiritual warfighters is intense. Indeed, our concern is more than working within the realm for only securing a temporary peace. Our fight, our war has eternal consequences. Therefore, it is mandatory that we know what His rule set entails. To know, we must read, study and listen, and commit our heart, mind, and soul to His plan. Once this is accomplished, we will better understand His goal. With understanding will He then

> Psalm 25:14 ... *show them that revere Him, His covenant*

His ROE, His plan. Covenant comes from the primary root word that means "to render clear," where absolutely zero uncertainties or doubts reside. Everything is clear. The CINC has just given me complete SA. His plan and ROE is listed in the Bible. Check it out:

> James 2:12 *So speak ye, and so do, as they that shall be judged by the law of liberty.*

What this means in our current vernacular language is: God has given us liberty. It's similar to being onboard ship for a few months and you're ready for it to pull into port. You are given liberty to do, see, and say what you desire. However, you've been trained to act responsibly. You've been advised to not go see certain places because being within the proximity of certain activities can be dangerous. You've been briefed on subjects you should avoid talking about. You Intel guys know the routine: neither confirm nor deny, eh?

Ok. I've digressed a little. God has not issued us a step-by-step journal to cover every moment in our lives. There is no Technical Order F117-33-1-2 that gives us a (you better accomplish it!) step by step procedural checklist for requiring us to accomplish steps 1-10 in (and only in) sequential order. He has given us the order to talk (*So speak ye,*) and ACT (*and so do,*) as free people. Free. Not acting like an unchained rebellious kid, when given an inch runs for miles like a scalded dog, only to become [once again] entangled in his "freedom." God has proclaimed the

ROE. It states to "Be on guard!" "WATCH!" We're to watch for Him; watch for our own team members; watch for others; watch for Satan and his troops.

We need to conduct ourselves in a responsible manner. One that re-presents Jesus, keeping our eyes and the eyes of our heart focused on Him. "On Earth, as it is in Heaven." If it won't happen in Heaven, then you better be darn well sure you don't proffer to it, or support that activity on Earth. Aye? This is the word of the Lord.

More specific instructions and procedures are located in the SPINS.

Chapter Twenty Nine—

Command by Negation

In a large theatre of operations, there can possibly be 100 or more aircraft (helicopters, fighter jets, wide body command and control "birds", plus the ever present commercial airliners trying to make a buck) flying at any one time. How in the world do Battle Managers keep control of this ever-changing environment? Actually, "changing" doesn't properly describe the environment and "dynamic" just doesn't even come close to cutting the mustard toward providing an adequate description.

Realize that fighters can travel faster than 400 miles per hour, helicopters can swarm like the Minnesota state bird on a hot, humid summer day and certain types of intelligence aircraft can watch the sound barrier try to catch up with them in their rear-view mirror.

Furthermore, in a hostile environment, it is not a good idea to have these aircraft circle the airport similar to the air traffic at JFK or LaGuardia on a busy day. That would make them all a very attractive target.

In addition to all of this ongoing air activity, you've got Ground Pounders (Army, Marines) with short range missiles poised on their shoulders actively searching the skies for a target. Although I'm absolutely positive that no missile shooter has ever been tempted or considered that the sooner they loose that rocket, the lighter their load becomes... but on the other hand, ...

These shooters do face a huge responsibility. They must defend an extremely small geographic area. Their targets are visibly seen for only a split second; and they have to process a lot of information and execute on the derived results nanoseconds after encountering the "split second." Talk about high stress and life or death pressure. Considering this, is it appropriate to compare their enthusiasm and motivation to defend their position by firing that missile, with a growing teenager told to "only eat that hot steaming steak when you become hungry"? You tell me.

There are not enough Battle Managers to tell each and every shooter and shooter related entity when to shoot, and at which specifically designated target. The Battle Managers also do not have that kind of accurate information readily available to them.

Furthermore, this procedure would not be effective in combat operations. It is a well-known and documented fact, that even the best war plans are trash-canned once the shooting begins. All those [formerly] laid back trigger squeezers and pickle-pushing button smashers (with names of "Ice", "Cold Steel", "Freeze", etc.) are now pumping hordes of adrenaline through their bodies at magnanimous rates. Their normally operative pressure-relief valves can't hold the flow of this "dam-busting" adrenaline surge, and the valves are now wide open. Is there a human alive that could keep a handle on all of these dudes simultaneously? Not!

Therefore, the Navy (this credit goes to the Navy because I first saw them execute Command by Negation during my time in joint operations) in order to more effectively use its (and the Marines') death wrenching capabilities, decided to control their frenzied warriors by exception.

Bear in mind, this is toe-to-toe combat, and in this extremely intense environment, "exception" is pretty durn-near the rule when describing anyone's personality. However, the Navy realized these guys would no-way be in the frame of mind to ask "Mother, may I..." engage this target before he shoots me. And hence, granted them the freedom to execute. Execute, only by first informing other combatants of their intentions. For example, "Rocket 31" signifies he's enroute to service target 11. If Rocket 31 does not receive a response from a designated source, Rocket is free and clear to proceed with his intentions. Only if Rocket is told "No" will he not proceed.

Now you might realize that there is going to be a lot of chatter and clatter on the radio and communication nets. How can anyone hear, listen, and discern everything that is going on? Isn't there a lot of traffic that gets "walked on" by others, or garbled due to the saturated radio frequency environment? Your query is well put. The Battle Managers have planned for this weakness. And their and my response to you is: "You're exactly right."

But although this methodology does have its weaknesses, its strengths and timeliness in keeping the Operations Tempo in "our director's" hands outweighs the other consideration of requiring participants to ask Mom's permission each and every time.

So what does this have to do with God? Does this mean we can act and attack as we desire until he whacks us with a baseball bat between the eyes? Not quite. God first used Command by Negation with the Israelis in the Old Testament (Numbers 30). When Moses was laying down the law [again] after taking a second census, God told him, "Moses, there's too much fanagling and wishy-washy stuff going on. Our troops need to have some responsibility for their own actions and this will accordingly ease your work-load, increase the efficiency, streamline the process, and make our operators more aware of the operational environment." Remember, the Israelis had just attacked several other nations' battle groups and kicked some serious butt. Their adrenaline was running high. They were still pumped from their success and calling each other by their callsigns: "SandMan," "WarDog," "Issachar the Invincible," etc.

God had to give Moses an effective environment to operate within because up until then Moses was the earthly CINC. Remember, we're talking about a population of over a million people here. All the tribal warfighting leaders and their subordinate staff members came direct to him for guidance, goals, discernment in the Rules of Engagement, Intelligence issues, etc. It was one heckuva demanding spot for Moses to keep his Situational Awareness of all these factors up and operating. True, Moses didn't have to worry too much about the air picture (airplanes and such) but he certainly had to have his stuff in one sock to command about three quarters of a million pumped up, adrenaline rich, and testosterone oozing warfighters. Make sense?

God, who is renowned for keeping His eye on the big picture, took Moses by the shoulder and said, "Hey Moses, We both know I've given y'all a detailed ROE to help you operate in this environment. Now is a good time to tell our warfighters that when they make a decision or take an oath, they will fulfill it unless you or one of their leaders negates their verbalized intentions. Matter of fact, this is probably a pretty good thing in raising up our future leaders and servants as well. Therefore, y'all need to apply this principle to your family lives, as well."

Blessed be the name of the Lord.

Chapter Thirty—

Special Instructions

Special Instructions, known as the SPINS, are an essential part of an issued command order. The SPINS address numerous areas covering procedural topics, such as how to engage the enemy in a certain environment or theater, to providing specific code words of wisdom to facilitate engagements. For example, spiritual SPINS might state:

Warfighters/Armor-bearers:
-Ensure Sword and Shield are at the ready, at all times.
-Fast lace, high-top boots required. Satanic snakes in OpArea
-Eye protection required on helmet. Devil's eye candy expected on ingress.

Code Words:
- Dad = JFC
- Purple Haze = Weapons Free, Positive Identification required.

Special Instructions are usually issued via hardcopy, i.e. printed out on paper, to ensure warfighters know exactly what actions to take when certain situations occur or when potential circumstances develop. For example, when aircraft are patrolling a certain area of airspace, (similar to a State Trooper patrolling a designated section of highway) and a flyer sees something approaching on the radar, a quick reference to the SPINS will determine what action(s) is required. For instance, one of the first instructed actions might require getting a positive identification on the approaching platform. If the type of aircraft is unknown, then under Positive ID, it is mandatory to first identify it. To positively determine whether the aircraft is a good or bad guy, or whether it's a neutral commercial airliner. The resulting identification will determine any follow-on actions.

Spiritual SPINS are located in numerous hardcopy publications also. It's absolutely essential to know the functional application of each of God's orders during times of crisis and combat. Without positive guidance and direction a warfighter can fall.

I've got to share a personal experience with you because it depicts how no matter what kind of interference or electro-magnetic anomalies occur, if Jesus wants His plan to be executed, then you can put $2 on that horse's nose, to win. It's going to happen. No doubt about it. No two ways around it.

Pastor Pa^{t}ul announced the 6:30pm healing service in today's sermon. I felt convicted [believed that Jesus was telling me] to attend it. Numerous excuses came up during the day for me not to attend, e.g. it was hot and Florida muggy. I was fixing and readjusting our sprinkler system. Not one of my favorite things to do, especially since I'm a believer if you don't water the grass, it won't grow, and hence, won't have to be cut. Argh-h-h. I was sweating like a pig and my temperament wasn't one I preferred to display in public, let alone to try and get regenerated back to a faithful servant status after so much frustration. (Sounds like I had my wires crossed, eh?)

It's amazing how my planned attendance was (I really believe this now) under continuous attack throughout the day. I even had to cut my Dad short from our weekly telephone conversation this evening at 6:10pm to get to church on time. Those of you who know my Dad, or have one like him, know that he can jawbone, delightfully, for hours upon end. I love you, Dad.

During the healing service, Pastor Pa⁺ul thought I was just there to run the sound board. The real reason I was there, however, was to observe a healing service. This was my first one, ever. Another reason for being present was to do some searching for myself and praying for others that needed help.

At the end of the service, as I was shutting down the soundboard, a lady I never met before came up to me and asked if I believed in prophetic senses. I said I wouldn't be smart enough to know if one happened, but yes, I believe they occur. She stated she had just had one from God. Would I like to hear it? I said yes.

She said God gave her the word "scribe" and told her to tell me, "scribe". I was immediately struck and almost started looking for my chair to sit down. She went on and explained the function and purpose for the Old Testament scribes. She also said God told her that I was having feelings similar to what Noah did before he built the ark. He, like me was fearful of what people would say about him. She said God is talking to me and that I was listening, to tell me that I'm doing right and I need to keep going. He will keep leading me. Then she asked if any of this made sense?

Wow! Joy, relief, amazement, awe, a conundrum of mixed and mismatched overwhelming emotions. I said that I had just started writing a book not even two weeks ago, and yes the analogy with Noah was certainly a match.

Now, let's review the complexity of these communication paths. Two people who had never set eyes on each other before; battling the typical hassles of daily life; travelling down separate unconnected pathways; directly impacted by weather, interference, [will] power outages, etc. God found a connector and plugged us in together to complete his [oh so] special instructions! Hallelujah Jehovah Nissi, the Conqueror!

The test of a true warfighter is to be able to:
Hear
Listen
Act

The ability to hear, listen and the willingness to step out and <u>act</u> on the instructions when they are received, mandates courage and loyalty, coupled with a <u>complete</u> and "unknowing" trust in Jesus' direction. Unknowing, because we might not know the reason. Don't be like the two-year old continually asking, "Why". Be more like the faithful servant and warfighter and… just DO it! according to His plan.

The lady who demonstrated these principles, and acted on God's direction definitely put a big check in each of these boxes that night. Are you getting all three boxes checked?

Chapter Thirty One—

JMTOP (Joint Multi-TADIL (Tactical Digital Information Link) Operating Procedures)

The JMTOP seeks to ensure the effective throughput of information in a tactical digital communications network. It assists in segregating certain types of information between participants and integrating other types of information among others.

Special Instructions are also issued via communication (voice or data) networks. Voice networks are good for relaying information in a very quick, timely manner. However, there are several inherent fallacies with voice networks that can impact operations. This is true, especially when they are used as the primary method for transmitting and receiving information. For example, a voice message can be hard to hear and therefore, not completely understood. Additionally, parts of the message might not make it to the intended recipient because of weather, equipment failure, or a host of other reasons.

On the other hand, data networks can be a more timely and useable form of communication. They host more benefits than weaknesses. For instance:

-The information is readily displayed on an operator's console.

- The information can be archived in a database for immediate retrieval at a later time.
- Information is not as likely to be misunderstood or garbled as voice, and
- Dissemination and distribution of the information can occur to a greater number of interested participants simultaneously.

However, similar to voice networks, these operational data networks can be also impacted by severe weather, equipment outages, and operator mistakes.

Similarly, God can also disseminate information via a communication network. To some, He can issue words of wisdom or knowledge. To others, He can come as the weather, e.g. a cool breeze, a burning fire, or a calm sea. Sometimes the words seem to be garbled or they are not completely understandable. Sometimes the meaning is unclear or only part of the message is clearly transmitted. When this happens, we need ask for a retransmission.

When requesting a "retrans" we go to someone who might have a better "receiver" for the comm net. Confirming partial or "garbled" messages with three different sources is always a good idea. In the physical world, this can be done by SATCOM; another receiver that gets the same type of information stream; or from a different source of information. In the spiritual realm, we immediately seek out the Ops Manual [the Bible] to ensure it does not trespass on His word. Then we can counsel with those in authority or our mentors, who can give us a verbal retrans, such as a person with the prophetic gift, or an intercessor. Then we can act based on the clarified message contents.

God can also use His data network to disseminate and distribute timely information. Our Special Instructions (SPINS) are also provided to us in hardcopy, the Bible. That is His primary source for disseminating timely, up-to-date information to His warfighters. However, there are occasions when He uses other alternative means (dreams, vision, music) to relay His information. Because like most networks, the pathways connecting them can be very complex and many times completely uncooperative: the servers (servants?) can go down, seemingly at will; connections can suddenly become loose, power surges can occur, interference from other sources can interrupt connectivity, etc.

When He is talking to you, then it's important, (No! It's mandatory!) to effectively hear Him, you have to listen up! If you're listening, then He'll ensure the complete communication gets through to you.

Chapter Thirty Two—

Interoperability

Most of the Department of Defense's (DoD) weapon, and command and control systems were designed for autonomous operation. Their main purpose was to protect the US and its friends from an attack by the [former] Warsaw Pact and Soviet Union. Under these conditions, these systems operated exceedingly well. Today, however, there is not a single definition for the "enemy". There is not a single big belly button to point to and call the "Evil Empire". The enemy can be defined in many diverse ways.

Similar to effectively combating the many enemies we have today, it is more probable that a mix of weapons systems, from all four military services, will be called upon to fight or stymie the enemy in order to achieve a declared victory or a termination in action.

This occurs because our focus has been distracted, we can't determine when a single act is important when it is taken as an isolated, independent activity. For a determination to be made, an act requires an association with other events.

Unfortunately, people are starting to define their own lives in this same manner. Worse yet, right and wrong is also heading down this path. Sin is becoming obscure in people's minds. It's a sin to lie, but OK if it's to protect someone's feelings. It's a sin to commit adultery, but sexual expression, and having an intimate loving relationship with someone you're not married to can be OK under many circumstances. (Excuse me while I spit!)

Integrating these diverse systems is where the problems really become evident because they just weren't intended to "play" with others. For example, let's say you have a building that is subject to potential break-ins and burglaries. You buy a guard dog for one purpose: to protect the contents inside the building. The dog operates exceedingly well. You let it free during the night and weekends, and it ensures nobody enters [or leaves] the building during its watch. It knows while you are present, it can snooze. But when you are gone, it's the dog's responsibility to Watch.

This is similar to the function of the autonomous DoD systems. The Rules of Engagement used to be explicit. All participants knew where the boundaries were, under what circumstances to engage, and even the most likely scenario to be encountered.

Now, after many years of operating under this ROE, your business is thriving and you need to open the building outside of normal operating hours. But your dog is used to sleeping during the day and you know that changing its hours to watch would be very stressful for him. An alternative would be to get another dog, but you really don't want another extremely large, ferocious dog because it eats too much and there's too much maintenance [clean up] required. So you decide on getting a Boa Constrictor because it only has to be fed occasionally and a Boa would surely make an intruder think twice. But you also hire your wife's brother because he only wants to work on weekends, during the day.

Can you envision the many different possible scenarios and outcomes that could occur? A deliveryman could arrive on Saturday morning, meet your wife's brother and everything would [initially] be OK. But maybe the dog didn't sleep well because the snake kept it up. Now the dog is grumpy, hears someone come in the building and ..

The joint environment is filled with these same types of [cats & dogs; sneaky snakes and operators] scenarios. Furthermore, most DoD systems use their own distinct language and unique uninterruptable algorithms to process and perform their decision-making functions. Translating and interpreting all these unique binary codes into a common, completely understandable language by all the other systems is a bold step. What do you think the odds are of this happening?...

Interoperability is the goal that would allow seamless, transparent operations to occur regardless of the mix or match of weapons systems or battle management devices. It is the key to maximizing combat TTPs and effectiveness. Similarly, our lives are a lot more complex than they were before. There are so many issues to contend with, so many more choices required. A lot of these areas seem to have no right or wrong, just different shades of gray. Many people define their present life as being dependent upon each situation they encounter.

Jesus wants the members of His church, His team to be completely interoperable also. I'm certain He couldn't give a hoot about the man-made imposed legalism and restraints that are used in some churches. He would want to keep things simple, for our simple minds. That's why when things get complicated and we feel like we're flat on our back, and we need a clear Line-of-Sight focal point... all we have to do is open our eyes and look [up]. "On earth as it is in heaven. My kingdom come. My Will be done." Focus on Jesus. Attain interoperability. Maximize your effectiveness. Integrate Jesus.

Operational integration exemplified:

Kurt Warner, Quarterback, St. Louis Rams
Super Bowl XXX Champions
Let's put first things first: Thank you Jesus! Go Rams!

Chapter Thirty Three—

Joint and Coalition Forces

We hear a lot about "joint this" and "joint that" whenever the Congressional Budget Office (CBO; see Glossary) talks about the military and efforts to save money. What does joint-ness have to do with saving money or fighting effectively? And furthermore, what's with the buzz about Combined and Coalition forces?

If we have joint forces, why do we want forces that are combined or coalesced?

Does combined mean they are inter-mixed, and joint means they are "hinged" together?

In order to keep us all singing from the same sheet of music, let's define and discriminate between the terms Joint and Coalition. Prior to massive budget cuts in the Department of Defense, the sister services (Army, Navy, Air Force, Marine Corps) bought, used and developed equipment and weapon systems as they [individually] determined necessary, without consulting the other sisters.

This will be addressed in the future section regarding Interoperability. When the first swing of the Congressional Budget Hatchet occurred, the sisters decided that coming up with a pre-determined "coherent" plan would be a good thing. It would show Congress they were getting along and acting civilly with each other. Rather than calling each other Jarhead, Squid, Zoomie, Grunt and other terms of affection, the different service members actually started using each other's real names and callsigns for greetings, e.g. "Hey, Ant." "What's goin' on Hound?" Et al. This simple act was called--- being "Joint."

Although there isn't any bureaucratic proof to it, I believe the term "joint" obtained its real derivation from the acquisition fighting-for-dollars warriors when they were locked up in the same room for extended periods of time battling and dialing for dollars. Thereby giving effect to the term "lockup", aka, the big house, the federal play pen, the "joint", etc. They needed to talk with each other to get their programs funded and their jobs accomplished.

Shoot, after a while, the sisters even decided it would show good will to play together, e.g. to run around carrying logs, rubber rafts, and to run full-tilt through the woods at night. Hence the derivation of the terms "exercise" and recognizably, "joint exercise."

When the politicians saw the great impact their hatchet had on the sisters, (they were, afterall, now playing together and calling each other names) they replaced the hatchet with Paul's double-edged axe. Paul Bunyon, that is. Fortuitous and bean-counting logic drove them to believe that if a little chop(?) is good, then jiminy whillickers, think of the resounding results a severing swoop right through meat and bone could produce. The result? The axe did swoop clean through. Severing appendages and brain cells from the composite body. Therefore, the answer to the above introductory question is "yes". A hinge is required to keep the joint forces hooked together.

OK, now that we've derided the term, joint. Hey, is that a typo? Don't you mean "derived"?

Heh, heh.

Have you ever noticed, in this politically correct age, a person's body language when they say, "There's no such thing as a stupid question"? My Dad said that once to me, but his fists were clenched and his jaw was clamped tighter than a pair of Robo-grips. Actually, my Gran'ma [bless her heart] had the best response...a good thump alongside the head, and a kick in the backside to return one back to reality.

Pressing on to Coalition or Combined Forces. For our purposes, these terms can be used interchangeably to follow the Keep It Simple (KISS) methodology. If you have ever watched sisters compete for anything, you can form a good picture of the coalition environment. Coalition forces refer to other nations that are our current friends who also have military sisters. And yes, some of these sisters have even redder hair than our own sisters. Ouch!

The consummate ideal is for our sisters and their sisters to exercise together. Everyone using their own gear, weapons, and other hardware in various stages of development, etc. Not only is it fun to get out and watch the sisters thrash around in the mud (now commercialized and televised), but it is also a great opportunity for each sister to update the others on who is doing what to whom, when, where, and how.

Without getting carried away, it is easily recognizable to visualize all the difficulties that can possibly occur in commanding and controlling all of these adrenaline-pumping redheaded sisters. I'll venture no further with that statement for fear of physical reprisal.

What does this have to do with God? And how do we as spiritual warfighters derive any benefit from this section? Did God employ joint operations? And what about coalition forces? And more importantly, does He still do that today?

Before we break into the Battle Management Command and Control (BMC2) functions. Let's take a grass-roots level look at the actual challenges the "tough-it-out" warfighters had to overcome then, just as they do now.

We've mentioned the different types of equipment that are used, as well as the mix of weaponry available from different nations today. The Israelis from the Old Testament had to deal with these same issues.

Like what? What different kinds of non-interoperable hardware could they possibly had to use? Afterall, spears are spears, and chariots are chariots, right? Allow me to address these questions while advising you by saying, "Lucky for you Gran'ma is relaxin' and doesn't want to be disturbed."

But just for your own personal edification, "parts is parts" only pertains to chickens. Part replacement for spears can depend on the length and circumference of the shaft, the weight, heft, and balance of the overall weapon, as well as the design and integration of the pointy end. I know you're just testing me because it's obvious one must consider the drag coefficient, the aerial worthiness, vibration testing (shake, rattle, and roll) during flight, etc. for each individual spear. Not to mention the type of wood and metal used and the process for joining the two dissimilar elements.

And then there's the chariot. Wow! Talk about a whole bunch of different variables involved with this: you got yur wheels [chrome, wood, gold], yur spokes [5-star mags or 100, 120 or 180 spoke], yur spear [already covered this one] and arrow carrier compartment, yur [wind]shield, reins holder, cup holder, et al …. You get the picture, I'm sure.

Now, as to God's use of joint forces. Let's look at Joshua when he deployed to Jericho. God made Joshua the Joint Forces Commander. True, he didn't have access to the Navy and Air Force components, as we know them today. But he did have a representation of Leathernecks (Marines) and infantry (Army) as well as a component of armored cavalry (charioteers, horsemen, etc.).

Other sister services included the priests (Levites) and musicians. His Marines and Army components paved the way and guarded the assemblage of Levites carrying the holy tabernacle as well as the musicians from danger. His Air Force component though unseen, was at very high altitude [off the radar scope] performing Combat Air Patrol missions. A key element in this battle. Some might disagree with me about the representation of these service components. And that's okay. You who disagree are allowed your own opinion…even if you are wrong. Anyhow, we've already talked about the complex factors that make joint operations difficult to execute smoothly (remember synchro-congruency?).

Joshua had it even tougher than our military has it today. We all know how musicians can be independent and hold really eccentric perceptions of what is important. Put yourself in Joshua's shoes. Guarding the musicians was an absolute necessity. To not only protect them from an enemy ambush, but just to keep them in line and also protect them from each other as well as the contingent of testosterone-pumping, weapons-bearing warriors leading the "fight" [heh, heh]!

Coalition forces can be exemplified by the kings and kingdoms of the Canaanites, Perizzites,

Hittites, Girgashites, Hivites, and Jebusites that assembled together to fight against Joshua and his army. They were immediately at a disadvantage because this was one of the very first times coalition forces were employed. As a matter of fact the CONOP for coalition forces wasn't even far enough along to assemble it into a draft copy. The Coalition Kings did have a good idea to employ the TEAM concept. They had a common goal: to destroy Joshua. However, they were previously only qualified for fighting for their own city and possessions. This lack of thorough BMC2 planning, practice and execution would impact the fighting abilities and motivations for their troops as we soon shall see.

Each king had his own perception of how to destroy Joshua and the Israelites. Their objectives were not directly correlated. Their priorities for fulfilling their objectives were not the same and furthermore their objectives were not synchro-congruently executed. Additionally, there wasn't any one king positioned to be the CINC. These guys were motivated to operate as a TEAM, but it couldn't [and didn't] flow all the way down to the troops that were slinging arrows and swinging swords. Therefore, their troops fell prone to questioning battle management decisions: "Why do we have to be point?" "Why are those other guys getting better food and beds than we are?" "Can we trust them to stand firm during an attack?"

Furthermore, as in any combined operation, the language element had to be overcome. The Department of Defense experiences the same challenges even today. For example, although the British believe they speak English, by George, it's not real English. It's the Queen's English. And have you ever conversed with an "English speaking" person from Wales or Scotland with a brogue? Get these English speaking people on a tactical radio with another English speaker from "Jersey" or from the hills of Georgia and test the waters of understanding there. I dare ya!

Battle Managers can overcome these disparities and seemingly trivial differences, with a check in the checklist box, or with a wink and a nod. But, to the tactical warfighter that has his hand on the hilt of the sword, these "trivial" differences can be the moment that determines life and death.

In combat, there is not enough time to ask, "Huh? What the heck did he say?" Let alone to have to, "Say what?" numerous times. A verbal exchange of this nature leads both warfighters to believe the other is completely incompetent and cannot be trusted to execute any action. The "Coalition Kings" were unaware of this critical combat performance component.

Joshua did not experience many of the BMC2 challenges the Coalition Kings encountered. He was working on a joint not a coalition level. His forces had exercised and been in combat together. They knew each others capabilities and weaknesses. But most importantly, their BMC2 structure was unfailingly recognized and adhered to. They all acknowledged the presence of only one Commander In Chief. One leader. Of course, that leader was the Almighty, Most High, God. But other than that, you can see how Joshua and the Israelis had the advantage of a more simplistic organizational chart. One his troops willingly accepted and were ready to follow

Referring back to the questions we asked above:
1. Does God still use joint and coalition forces today?

2. And more importantly, how do we as spiritual warfighters derive any benefit from this dissertation on joint and coalition forces?

Yes, to the first question. God is using joint and coalition forces to fight His battles today. The crumbling of the Berlin Wall, the decomposition of the Soviet States are but two examples of joint and coalition forces executing His plan. Other plans are in the initial stages of execution. Look toward Asia for serious combating of the OPFOR as well as in other areas throughout the Middle and Near East.

And Yes also, to the second question. We, as spiritual warriors, must be adept at exercising and joining our combined and coalition compatriots in taking His fight to Satan. We need to be practiced and experienced in the spiritual BMC2. To rely on each other though there are language differences. To stand toe-to-toe in taking back what is rightfully His. We already have the simplified organizational chart (org chart) with the One CINC. We just need to ready ourselves for the differences the OPFOR will attempt to exploit as weaknesses in our endeavors to successfully attack his strongholds!

Chapter Thirty Four—

Integration – The Key

The Department of Defense is still working on integrating all of its current hardware, software, and people. They are working on assuring their future equipment will also be compatible with the hardware and software in existence (joint and coalition) as well as that in developmental stages.

God is also working on integrating all the current disparate parts of His church (Baptists, Methodists, Lutherans, Catholics, etc.) and His body to operate in a more effective manner. To operate as a well oiled combat oriented machine. To engage the enemy from a point of vantage. His principle and directions remain the same as when He pulled Moses aside to talk with him.

Namely, seek Him steadfastly, with your whole heart. Trash your narrow field-of-view autonomy for His CTP on seamless integrated operations. Why? What's the real benefit?

- Total 3-D coverage.
- Complete SA, under all circumstances.
- Maximum weapons engagement capabilities.
- Zero fratricides.
- Clear and distinctly stipulated ROE.
- No breakdown in communications.
- No net over-loading.
- Maneuver occurs in a choreographed, practiced, anticipated manner.

- Engaging the enemy in a timed, synchronized attack!
- Winners, no losers. Take no prisoners. Hooah.

Chapter Thirty Five—

A War Song:
Ode to the Warfighter

> *2Thes 3:3 But the Lord is faithful, and He will strengthen and protect you from the evil one!*

Psalms 23 is not usually thought of, or considered, as representing an operational warfighting environment. Most people look to this chapter as a peaceful interlude for walking with Jesus. Look again! This is not a mamsy-pamsy, listen-to-the-birds-chirping, the bees buzzing, and enjoying the gentile, aromatic effervescence of blooming flowers along the pathways. No. This is a war-psalm, a rendition from an aged warrior, depicting a confident, aggressive warfighter, taking a death-defying, brazenly-bold walk through the most sinister and evil place in all the heavens and worlds, outside of Hell itself.

Allow me to further enhance your situational awareness to the immediate environment.

> *[1] The Lord is my shepherd; I shall not want.*

This one short statement bears all the elements we've already discussed in the previous sections. It's obvious this person is a warfighter, graduated from Advanced Training and Tech School. Consider the element, Subordination of Self in the phrase "He is my leader." The warfighter acknowledges he is on a team and he is willing to follow the CINC's Rules of Engagement. Hence, discipline and responsibility are also self-evident. Furthermore, the warfighter states, with confidence, that all his present and future needs, and requirements are already met. He knows the Commander will equip him better, and with more gear (armor, communication equipment, logistics, etc.) than he could ever think of asking. He will properly equip him for any encounter on the road ahead.

[2] He maketh me to lie down in green pastures;

Did you catch the resistance factor here? The Commander "ordered" the warfighter to catch some R&R (Rest and Relaxation). God knows our physical, emotional, and mental limits. Just like in the Old Testament, He ordered the Israeli's to work six days and chill out on the seventh: To bask in God's warmth and glory. So it is here. God knows what is coming up around the corner. This is a preparation step to rejuvenate our strengths, allow our wounds to heal, to enjoy His presence and get closer to Him.

he leadeth me beside the still waters.

Either this warfighter has already gone through some really stressing times, or the Lord must know of a tough upcoming test for this guy. He's pulling out all the stops to ensure the warfighter is completely rejuvenated and in tip-top condition. (By the way, do you think they had hot mud-baths back then?)

[3] He restoreth my soul;

This can only be accomplished by complete subordination of self. By keeping one's complete, continuous, undivided attention on Jesus. Envision the warrior walking side by side with Jesus. Each has an arm around the other's shoulder. Each kinda leaning on each other, ambling along the lakeside, laughing, shouting and joking around. Hey, did you see that? Jesus got the warfighter with a belly punch. He's got him in a headlock. Look, He's giving him a nougie! Who says our Lord doesn't have a sense of humor? The warfighter is completely enthralled and basking in His presence. Pure, utterly relaxing, joy and satisfaction.

> *He leadeth me in the paths of righteousness, for His name's sake.*

God wants the warfighter to realize there is more to learn and absorb regarding His holiness. God is showing the warfighter the unquestionable Truth, the perfect Light. Notice that there isn't a compare and contrast educational effort going on here. God doesn't take evil and say, "Now don't do this and don't do that." [Digress: Have you ever been to a public beach or park? Did you see the sign that says: No swimming, no sailing, no pets, no food, no drink, no running, no radios, no sports equipment.... no fun?] The CINC shows the warfighter what is right and what needs to be done. The "why" is made self-evident. The warfighter now knows the purpose for any encountered challenge. He's pumped! He's ready to get back in action! Thank you Lord for the R&R. Thanks for the walk & talk. Now, I've been in the safety of your fortress for too long. It's time for me to get back out there and accomplish more of your objectives.

As the warfighter leaves the pleasant rolling hills of green pasture land, the burbling brooks, streams and valleys fade from his sight. The birds soaring in the clear sky, the fat-bodied bees and butterflies flitting among the flowers also diminish. The sounds that God's happy creatures make, also wither away....

There, in the distance, a massive wall arises, as far as the eye can see, heavily fortified, reinforced with armored abutments, electro-optics, sensors, unidentifiable hosts of evil spirits, physical entities, and "bodies" [neither physical nor spiritual, but a category that nevertheless falls somewhere in between]. A huge portal maybe 60 feet high by 27 feet wide is at the entrance for those that dare approach. It's heavily gated, has reflective armor mounted on its walls and is reinforced with high-strength concrete. It's been sprayed with a chemical that encourages the growth of moss and algae for blending into the dense forest/jungle that surrounds the wall. Over the top of the portal is an arch that bears these words constructed from heavy, rusted iron rods:

Valley of Shadows & Death

The sound of absolute, eerie quiet is washed in death. A pervasive sense of evil is mixed in with the foreknowledge that an imminent encounter is in preparation for your presence. (Remember 1Peter 5:8b ...Your opponent, the devil prowls around like a roaring lion in search of someone to devour. This is his headquarters. Hell on earth.) Sensors are monitoring your every physical twitch and move; your thoughts are being broadcast to every "living being" on the other side. Waiting, watching, rehearsing the attack on your weaknesses, subverting your strengths, altering your perception by deception, and ending your spiritual existence. It is known that most will go to any length to completely avoid heading in the direction toward the Valley. Only a few will even dare look toward the wall. Fewer still will have the courage to cast their gaze and step up to the "gate".

What's this? There's one now. Approaching the gate, poised for any kind of booby trap, ambush, or direct frontal assault. He's standing there ready. Up front and very personal at the gate leading into the entrance for the Valley.
His lips are moving. What's he saying?

[4] YES! I'm walking through the Valley of Shadows & Death. I have No Fear! Jesus, I know you're with me.

This verse is screaming of pure strength, courage and bravery. All these virtues are represented in this one, single verse. Look at it closer:

YES!
A demanding shouting of joy. Yelling for encouragement. Whooping it up for an imminent [warring] action. This person has a "Fear This" sticker on his sword, a No Fear tattoo on his arm and knows he is completely outfitted (armor and weaponry) directly by 3n1, Incorporated (Father, Son, Holy Spirit).

I'm walking through
We're talking back straight, moving along at an even, steady, gait. Confidence squirting out of the pores of his skin. Ready for action. Feelin' froggy? Then, jump!

the Valley of Shadows and Death.

Let's pull this apart. A valley is generally a geographically low point in elevation, surrounded by mountains or high steep hills. In any event, one's Line-of Sight (LOS) is strictly curtailed. It's difficult to see for a distance in any direction (front, back, or sides). Dense vegetation, dim light. The only clear view is up. Hmm-m-m. How appropriate. When things are crowding in on you, and you can barely see beyond your nose, a simple action is all that's required.... Look up [to Him].

Moving along, a shadow can only exist if some-thing is present. The shadows in this Valley are moving, lurking; the swishing sounds of grass and brush being swept aside; twigs snapping; clicking of metal against metal; grunts, groans, running... caused by entities or beings, spirits or physically present forms laying in wait for you to trip, stumble, or fall. Some are lurking, just waiting for a moment of weakness or lackadaisical attitude. Others are merely looking out of the corner of their eye. Still others are predators, walking a parallel path to you, like a lion waiting for just the right moment to attack and devour his prey. And then a few will even take a bold aggressive stance similar to a wrestler, his face in yours, jostling for position, feinting moves, to catch you off balance in order to spear you. But the warfighter is walking through this pit of terror, similar to the Terminator: head up, ready, confident with every movement.

> Now look at verse 5,
> *[5] God is preparing a table before me in the presence of my enemies;*

What why would God do this to anyone? Wasn't it just a couple of chapters back that He told us not to associate with the enemy? And now we're allowing them to attend a feast on our behalf?

OK. Think this one over. Here's the setting: Picture a horseshoe of tables placed together, two rows of tables end-to-end, perpendicular to the head table. The head table is actually comprised of three tables placed end to end. It's brimming with fountains of fresh fruit, roasted suckling pigs, lamb, duck, choice cuts of beef and venison; crystal & gold goblets and punch bowls, all filled; streams of light reflecting from hanging chandeliers; intricately decorated fine china and solid gold and silver flatware set on the table. Two world-renowned chefs attend the table. Two lines of attendees awaiting the arrival for the head table. There's only one seat positioned in the center. It is an unidentified position. Neither the guests nor the management can indicate their knowledge for the expected person.

Into the banquet hall walks the same warfighter that traversed through the Valley of Shadows and Death. His enemies are aghast. Rather than an uproar of rage and rejection, there is a deathly quiet in the banquet hall. Fear, plotting, and perceived retribution ominously fill the atmosphere. However, this warfighter is not now predisposed to fight, although he is also not afraid of his currently confronted enemies of God and of his self. This feast is in honor of the relationship existing between the warfighter and God. If the warfighter didn't believe or didn't trust in Jesus [His overall command and control], the guest of honor wouldn't show up. Correct?

God has anointed my head with oil
For this warfighter knows he is publicly blessed by Jehovah Nissi (The Conqueror). God will protect him in all his actions, as long as he follows His

directions. For God has promised him His unfailing love, care, and attention.

My cup runs over

Runs over with what? With the gifts (armor, weaponry, courage, and teammates) that God provides. Pure joy, grace, power and authority are given to the warfighter by Him, the Almighty. Every human need, hope, and desire is washed away by His "ver abundant" provisions. Jehovah Jireh, our Provider!

[6] Surely, goodness and unfailing love shall follow me

Read this "surely" as. "It's a fact, Jack!" The shall is a legal term meaning: Must, a requirement, "You gotta do it!"

all the days of my life

This is not a temporary vacation spot on the beach. This is for each and every day. For each and every breath and heart beat. For *ever*.

and I shall dwell

There's that "shall" word again. Note the word "dwell." Have you ever stayed with friends on a vacation? You probably were comfortable staying with them, but it just wasn't home. Right? Dwell means: to reside; to occupy. It implies a long-term condition.

in the house of the Lord forever.

Home sweet home. At last. Amen.

Courage? Bravery? Confidence? Talk the talk. Walk the walk. Stay true to the course Jesus has laid out for you. Use the footprints Jesus has put in your path. Success, long-awaited honor and freedom await you at the end of the seemingly darkest moments.

Combat Missions

Chapter Thirty Six—

Combat Search and Rescue

Combat Search and Rescue (CSAR) is one of the most up-front, in-your-face dangerous, high-risk, high-yield operations performed in a combat environment. This operation only occurs when one of our fellow team members has fallen. Fallen not necessarily into the hands of the enemy, but certainly within their proximity, in their theater of operations, in their backyard. The riskiest part about this venture is the enemy knows one of our members is down. They know his approximate location. They know they have the advantage. Our downed team member is disadvantaged psychologically, logistically, emotionally, potentially disoriented, physically disabled and out-gunned. The bad guys know how much we revere the life of our team member. They will rush to the location to attempt the initial intercept and set ambushes for the expected CSAR crewmembers. They definitely have the "home advantage," and time is on their side. Even so,

> *They will fight against you, but they shall not overcome you, because I am with you to rescue you, says the Lord.* Jeremiah 1:19

CSAR is an important, absolutely necessary mission. It is also an inherently dangerous mission. Recognizing these dangers is adamant in performing the CSAR mission. Be on guard!

Watch! This is not just the "watch" one says to suggest a quick glance at something: "Hey, look at the 20" wheels on that GTI." It is the **WATCH!** given to a guard dog to protect at all cost a given object. It is the **WATCH!** of a pilot sitting in the cockpit on Victor Alert: armaments hot, engines running, aircraft standing on the end of runway awaiting the "Go" word.

The Lord wants us to get out of His fortress. He wants us to go outside of the secured perimeter. He wants us to get into combat! If He didn't desire these things, why would He say that [if we get in too deep, or out-numbered] He will rescue us? Is He going to perform a CSAR behind His own fortress walls? Get real. He wants to show us how important we are to Him, at all costs. As He did on the cross. Ok? Make sense?

> *Convince some who doubt, but save others by snatching them from the fire;* Jude 22

This is the prevalent operand for CSAR. Quick in and out. Snatching teammates from the enemy. But there are times when we receive tasking to even snatch up people perceived to be the enemy; to be saved by us. On our part, time is definitely of the essence. All players mandate a genuine sense of urgency. All information gathering is focused on timely data. Our attention is drilled to the present. Not tomorrow, not this evening, not yesterday or the day before, but right now. Pronto.

> *[23] on still others have pity*

Our God is a merciful God. He will not remain angry forever.

> *mingled with great caution,*

However, don't become indistinguishable from the enemy. This mission entails potentially deadly action. Be on guard. Remain on high alert!

> *loathing even the clothing that has been polluted by their sensuality.*

It is not OK to accept the sinful ways or evil exploits of Satan. Recognize him and his troops for what they do, for their plans to execute their mission against Jesus.

As warfighters under continual attack, we will come under direct fire. Under these circumstances, even we might lose a tread, flame an engine out, veer off the road, somehow become "disoriented" and require a CSAR operation to bring us back. But we can rest assured, Jesus has already prepared the Op for rescuing us.

> 2 Peter 2:9 *If we confess our sins, He is faithful and just*

Please make absolute cognizance that this is present tense. Jesus isn't talking about tomorrow or yesterday. His message is for the present, right now. He states, "Give me the timely information to determine what's going on." I'll use it

> *to forgive our sins and to cleanse*

Well, what's the first form of assistance required after rescue? Probably first aid, eh? Believe me, Jesus has plenty of Neosporin, Bacitracin, and Band-Aids readily available in his first aid kit. The kit is one of those "Ready Upon Request" gadgets. It takes all the dirt, grease, blood [and sin] away and cleans

> *us from all unrighteousness.*

Talk about a faithful, loyal, and trustworthy medic. His dispensary is always full. Always present at your side. All you have to do is call out. No push-to-talk radio required. No flare to pop, no beacon to activate. It's immediate. You call; He's there. Pronto.

Chapter Thirty Seven—

PsyOps/CCD

Psychological Operations (PsyOps) Camouflage, Concealment, and Deception (CCD) are generally referred to as "mind games" and other "sneaky stuff" respectively. These referrals make sense, don't they? PsyOps has been used effectively in numerous wars, conflicts, and outbreaks of violence. There are numerous activities that can be employed using PsyOps. For instance, one PsyOps activity you probably remember was the Tokyo Rose radio show. A take-off from Merv Griffin during WWII. Her pop, be-bop music had the troops dancing in the streets. Her message of defeat undoubtedly put questions in some of the troops minds, but she unexpectedly also put a lot of calcium in the backbones of our front-line fighting guys. Hooah!

Another typical PsyOps operation can be dropping papers from high flying "cargo" type aircraft. No, the papers aren't dropped in pallets to assimilate bomb drops. However, this is where the word "flyers" comes from. The aircraft have to be high enough to stay out of range of small arms, rockets, and artillery that they might encounter because they are flying directly over "Bad-guy" land. At a predesignated geographical location, the loosely bundled papers, thousands of them, are pushed out of the aircraft to float and disperse in all directions for everyone on the ground to take and dispense of properly, once their labor union gives them their 10-minute coffee break.

The Bad-guy troops and civilians then go around looking for the flyers and hoping for that 3-day free vacation in Aruba or Disneyland. However, what they find is a message similar to this, "Why don't you go back home? You're going to lose this war. Your union isn't going to pay you for your work. You won't be able to buy your girlfriend dinner at the Olive Garden for a long, long time and she'll be really, really mad at you. Go home, forget about your tax rate. We'll drop you root beer and peanuts on our next fly-by, instead of Mk82s and 84s." (Note: The Mk 82s and 84s definitely go "boom" in the night!). Can you imagine the clamor this raises when people realize there is a lot of truth in that message? Can you also imagine how angry the local environmentalists are from all this littering?

Camouflage, concealment, and deception (CCD) lends itself to not only the visual misrepresentation of an entity, but also borders on the manipulation of "perceived" information, leading to Dis-information... Can you read that sentence again, and tell me what it means? Maybe an example would help establish a little SA. Here ya go:

The most obvious form of CCD is camouflage, familiarly called camo. Hunters use camo clothing to conceal their presence in the woods. The Army uses camo paint schemes [effectively] to hide huge pieces of artillery in scrawny stands of trees (concealment).

I gotta tell you this story. I worked in [the former] West Berlin, Germany for a few years. About 2-3 times a week, instead of riding the bus to work, I'd either run or ride my bike through the Berlin forest for a great workout. About 10km each way. On one of those "run to work" days, I lost my gym locker key. Duh-h. So I decided to take a pleasant stroll back home through the woods. Man, it was a beautiful afternoon. The sun was shining, the birds were chirping. There were wild fuzzy animals crashing through the bushes (Agh! Please don't be a wild boar, Omigosh!) Then.... BANG! Right smack dab in front of me. Not 50 feet away. This HUGE British tank parked right alongside the trail. My whole being must have literally done a "shock-the-body" dance because the 'Brits were just hooting and howling from my antics. All I know is that CCD, and that paint job was the best I have ever seen. That's my story, and I'm sticking to it.

Moving along to the last of the trilogy items, Deception. Teenagers tend to use deception quite frequently and some very effectively. This can be accomplished by dressing in camo garb, applying camo "goo" to their faces, and/or dressing in odd rags and bags in order to conceal their activities from their parents. Just kidding. Most teenagers are not [too] deceiving, they're just----teenagers. A finer example of deception is the little dog in the back window. You know, the dog whose head always bounces up and down. It is deceptively answering everyone's questions, e.g.:

Person #1: "Isn't that cute?"
Dog: Yes.
Person #2: "Isn't that stupid?"
Dog: Yes.
Person #3: "Why would anyone put one of those stupid things in their car?"
Dog: Yes.

We know that Satan is the Great Counterfeiter. He can produce nothing that is good. All he can do is alter good for counterfeiting purposes. He is the master of deception, disguise and lies. Let's illustrate with a few quick holy examples:

Christmas: The birth of our Lord. An absolutely most holy day to rejoice and celebrate our God's journey to set us free. The Counterfeit: Commercialization, desire for more materialism, fake personage (Santa Claus) to replace Jesus (sorry about that kids, but its true).

Easter: Jesus replaced by some stupid animal that is known for high sexual activity. Enuf said.

All Saints Day: Day of Reformation. Counterfeited with Halloween spooks, goblins, spirit of fear, etc.

St. Patrick's Day: When Christianity kicked the paganists butt as the Truth. Counterfeited by becoming a modern day of drunkenness and debauchery.

These are relevant, pertinent examples of deception at its highest. Ask any spiritual warrior with an intel background.

Check out what Peter had to say about CCD. There are already in existence false prophets and "teachers" that are positioned to employ CCD for Satan's purposes. They are described as:

> 2Pet 2:10... *those who yield to fleshly desires, indulge in polluting passions, and despise authority. Bold [&] headstrong..., they have no qualms at libeling glorious beings,... [12]...likeirrational brutes... [13]...Revelry during the day is their idea of enjoyment; ...they stuff themselves at your table. [14] ...their appetite for sin is never satisfied. They lure unsteady souls. Their hearts are practiced in greed... [18] ... they utter arrogant nonsense, they entice,...*

These people certainly have the ability to put themselves into positions of authority as a professional, an expert, an experienced writer, analyst, professor, scientist, etc. We are cautioned and put on alert, that 2Pet 3:16b-17

> *The untaught and unsteady twist those* [biblical] *writings, as they do the other Scriptures... You therefore,...*[warfighters!], *are forewarned, be on your guard(!) so that you may not be carried away by* [these] *...lawless,* [rogues, brigands, and hose-bags who pose as professionals and societal mentors] *and lose your own stability;*

Cutting to the chase, fellow warfighters, DON'T stroll through the woods with your senses lulled (and your armor dulled) by peaceful serenity. Don't let the business end of a 50-ton tank in your face or even worse, the enemy "stuffing themselves" at your table jolt you back to reality!

As a matter of fact, we as spiritual warfighters have an even greater ability to use PsyOps and CCD against the enemy. As a team, we can use unpredictability and daring in our warring tactics.

When we maneuver in an unpredictable and daring manner, the enemy is fraught (that is a composite word blended from "freaked out" and "caught" [with his pants down]) with disarray and confusion. When we execute these TTPs, the result is a complete surprise of the enemy. It leaves them fearful. It leaves them questioning what is going to happen next.

It leverages the standard calculated risk tables established on combat engagement and tips the enemy completely off-center. Hence, it greatly reduces our own risk factors and yields even greater benefits.

Plus it puts a huge smile on our (and the Commander's) face knowing that we have totally "fraught" the enemy and kicked their composite butts!

Chapter Thirty Eight—

Sabotage/Espionage

Destruction, lies, spies, and more bad guys. Having bad guys do bad things to the good guys camp. Or even worse, enlisting good guys to do bad things to their own camp. Sometimes unknowingly, sometimes belittling the deed as very minute or miniscule. Always, yes always, attempting to put another crack in the foundation of the team. The Bible states

> *Woe to the shepherds who destroy and scatter the sheep of My pasture...you have scattered My sheep and driven them away and have not tended them. Look! I on my part will attend to you for the evil of your doings, says the Lord.* Jeremiah 23:1-2

Whoa. Back the truck up! This is serious business. Karl Marx could be known as one of the great spiritual saboteurs. His often quoted statement that "religion is the placebo of the masses" has been heralded by many atheists, and governmental and civil leaders. To Karl, religion merely offered the people hope without any substance. It made them lethargic and not suitable to join and develop his concept of the "working class". It tears me up to have to tell you this, Karl. But man, you really missed the boat here. If Karl would have only stopped, looked, and listened, he could have realized that

> Romans 1:19 *whatever can be known regarding God is evident to them, for God has shown it to them. [20] From the creation of the world His invisible qualities...have been made visible and have been understood through His handiwork.*

Jesus is by no means a placebo. If anything He is the polar opposite to that. He is a highly potent spiritual antioxidant; providing focus for what is important in this life. He's the anti-virus to Satan and those who serve him, either willingly or unwittingly. Filled with energy, enthusiasm, and compassion for all His troops, Jesus is our active guardian, our BMC4I, our JFC. He is there with us, to war against Satan, his servants, demons, and evil ways.

The saboteurs who attempt to suppress the Truth through government totalitarianism, dictatorships, atheism, and other means,

> *...indulged in their speculations until their stupid minds were all in the dark.* Romans 1:19

Recognize this. Karl was an intelligent person by earth's standards. If he took an IQ test, I'm confident to say he would have placed in the level above dumb, quite easily. However, by spiritual or divine standards, [my opinion:] poor Karl was not only dumb, he was stupid.

> *[22] Claiming to be wise, they became foolish.*

Hey Karl! Sounds to me like you've been taking too much of your own "medicine." Was Forest Gump right, or what [e.g. Stupid is, as stupid does.]?

> *[24] Therefore God gave them up... [25]* [Because] *they altered God's truth into falsehood...[26] ... God abandoned them...*

Wow, talk about a powerful act. God must've looked at these guys, rolled His eyes back, despondently shook His head, turned His back, and walked away. Wow! Can you imagine how "dark," dark is without God?

> *[32]While knowing God's ordinance*

His directions, His orders,

> *that those practicing such things deserve death,*

Basically these guys are spiritual criminals serving a "life" sentence, while they're still on earth

> *they not only practice them but even give their approval to those who do them.*

Similar to the aforementioned CCD'ers, they sell themselves as professionals, the cultural elite, "free" thinkers. They not only practice, but teach, instruct, and cajole others into taking up their ways. Chipping away at the foundation in order to place a pack [just a small pack mind you] of C4 for use at a more appropriate time.

Be on guard. Keep your armor up, on, and operating. These, are dangerous times. These, do not wear the uniform of a combat warfighter. These, speak of peace while keeping their weapons concealed and ready. These, attempt to draw you in by their "wisdom" and smile. These, smile and freely shake hands. Beware! These, are now in control of your trigger finger.

OK, I submit. Blanca reminded me that she is a South Paw. She's safe from the handshaking reference above. Yes, Jesus knows we need more South Paws. Thanx, dear.

Chapter Thirty Nine—

Servicing the Target

Servicing the target is generally thought of as putting fire and steel on target to totally obliterate it, to transform it into a smoking hole. We saw this day after day from out-briefings during Desert Shield/Desert Storm. But there are numerous other options available when it comes to servicing a target, such as exploitation, disruption, isolation, etc. These other options must always be kept in mind, especially when the target requires CSAR as previously discussed.

However, one constant that remains under any condition when servicing a target is the sense of urgency. Notice how the Old Testament Passover was celebrated:

> Exodus 12:11 *Thus shall ye eat it; with your loins girded, your shoes on your feet,*
> *and your staff in your hand; and ye shall eat it in haste.*

In the day the blood was applied, they had to be equipped for a journey, for that day was for them, the threshold of a journey. It was not just to be a critical experience, one to be enjoyed and then forgotten, or something ecstatic, which would then become a fond memory of the past. The Passover was to be the beginning---the means, not the end! From this day they could never be the same again. They were to embark upon a journey. Correlate this with training. Understand the sense of urgency invoked in accomplishing extremely critical actions. Preparation. On guard. The sense of urgency is prevalent in God-leading history. Where in the Bible does he tell his followers to slack off? To chill out?

When Jesus calls. We [must] respond immediately. The disciples literally dropped their fishing nets right there and followed Him. They didn't rinse the nets off, hang them up to dry, fold them up or tell anyone else to clean up from the end of the day's work. They didn't plan for the possibility of coming back to fish tomorrow, the next week, or the next month. They completely submitted themselves right then and there, to follow Jesus. To heck with everything else. It's not important. We're hanging with the Master. Like in the Old Testament, the nation of Israel was ready to respond at the sound of His voice. God says, "Go." The whole entire nation "Went." No questions; no caveats. We're outta here. Are we able to do that today? Or would our response be: "Wait until half-time, OK?" "Can I just finish this last cross stitch?" "Let me call Uncle Joe and Aunt Frieda first. The dogs have to be fed."

Satan is a devious, tactics oriented professional. The TTPs used by him are not new. They are all based upon one principle, sin. Jesus has determined that there is only one ultimately correct option to servicing Satan, the target. Destruction, complete obliteration, ashes to ashes, dust to dust. But the pathway leading to his destruction and to the destruction of his work, might demand different responses, initially.

John states in 1 John 3:8 that
The

This is not pronounced, "the." The correct pronunciation of this word is "the-e-e," as in "The-e-e" primary, the-e-e-e one, the-e-e main, the-e-e fundamental

reason the Son of God appeared was to destroy the devil's work!

No further explanation required here, eh?

Courses of Action

Chapter Forty—

Action

"Of course, I believe it. I've seen it done a hundred times before. It's easy. Just point and shoot." How many times have we said, "It's easy." or "Even I can do that. No problemo, dude." To something we've never really, actually experienced. Ok, maybe we experienced something [kinda sorta] similar to it. Whereby we can make a logical leap for doing it, but yet, still not experiencing the actual task, the real McCoy. For instance, we've all seen a bullfight, right? It looks easy. We've seen the matador jaunt out with his cape, to swirl and twirl before the bull. Anyone can do that; it's just a matter of timing. Did you evaluate this "experience" by watching it on TV? Or as an observer in the grandstands? Or were you seeing it from the eyes of the matador, facing the 2-ton bull, toe-to-toe, in the combat zone? Do you think it really makes a difference?

I remember firing my first hundred pistol rounds for the Marksman badge. Prior to this, I was a gunsmith and an avid pistol hunter. A major part of my four basic food groups was cordite. I believed I could achieve the Marksman medal because I had fired 10s and 9s consistently for many years. [OK. I also fired 7s. Give me a break, all right?] Others on the firing line also believed they could shoot Marksman. But they didn't [yet] have the experience. Some had never even fired a pistol. But, hey! It looked easy. Look how close the targets are. Point, shoot, score. Left handed, right handed, shoot-move-shoot. However, when the pistol barks, there's no turning back. It's game time. Winner or loser. There's nothing in between.

Isn't it curious that "believing" doesn't necessarily transform itself into, or directly correlate with, successful completed action? Sometimes our "belief" is actually just a strong desire or even sometimes just a wish. But without the actual physically-relational experience, our desires [wishes] remain just that, desires of inaction, (i.e. couch potato, deadhead, veggie, wannabe). A positive action and most often a physical encounter is required to move us from the "belief" arena into the "faith" arena. As James states in

> James 1:22 *But be doers of the word, and not deluders of yourselves by merely listening.*

Although I don't think James was renowned as the local mathematician, let me attempt to explain this principle to you logically, in a mathematical manner. Faith can be depicted by the Additive Theorem $(a + b = c)$, as:

Belief + Action = Faith

Belief is the internal mechanism of listening, understanding, desiring, or wishing something without employing any type of action to accomplish or secure it. It is "head knowledge." Both elements, i.e. belief and action are required to garner the resultant faith. Take away either element (Belief or Action) and Faith can NOT exist. The result instead, is merely lip service. The non-believing or inactive Intellect will say: "Oh, I know that already." Or, "Yes, I heard that and I believe it." But what it all pans out to, plain and simple, is SPIT. So don't give me your stinkin' phony intellect and tongue (SPIT). Just do it or g'it out of my face!

Please note James' determination in pointing out the "word," and not the "Word." This is the authentication code for specifically denoting the spoken word, vice the written Word. God's [spoken] word can be given to us by those who have authority over us. More frequently it can also be given by our present day prophets and apostles. These enable us to become more aware of currently revealed Christian principles, new strengths, talents, gifts, and understanding. James says, "Put it into practice! Don't sit on it! Be a Do-er! Act. Execute!" The Battle Manager observes the war for better Situational Awareness. We the warfighters, fight the fight. Remember, we humans are on the battlefield. We're engaging the enemy in combat. If we're only watching, we are overcome and die a disgraceful death of cowardice/fear.

James 1:23 *for whoever hears the message without acting upon it is similar to the man who observes his own face in a mirror.*
Ugh! Now, I've got to admit this example is easy for me to avoid. I look at myself as little as possible. We all know an ugly mug when we see one. To me it's someone else's problem. I don't have to look at this mug except to scratch the beard off every morning. However, some of y'all have to look at me for extended periods of time. [Condolences.] But a person who contemplates his own mug in the mirror; fully studying himself for just the right clipping of hair (ear, nose, eyebrows, and neck), the closeness in shave, and overall "lookin' good, dude" qualities doesn't have his mind on what's important, i.e. the present battle. His Situational

Awareness is centered on self, not on fighting for Jesus or helping out his teammates. He's not only a detriment to himself, but also to everyone with him on the battlefield.

If we or one of our team members hears a Word of Knowledge or Wisdom and doesn't act on it, that could be considered as direct insubordination; a blatant disregard for the CINC. Defying His order.

> James 2:14 *What is the use for anyone to say* [we] *have faith, if* [we] *fail to act on it? [Our] faith cannot save [us], can it? [17]* [No way] *Exactly so, faith that does not work is---dead.*

How can you say you trust the CINC when He gives you a direct order and all you give Him is lip service (SPIT)? You gotta pull the trigger to shoot the enemy! Just having the weapon or wearing the armor, and "believing" (or is it actually hoping?) it will work as designed isn't good enough. It has to be used. Executed per its function. For example, if you are given the gift of prophecy or healing and you keep it to yourself. You don't use it to benefit others. What good is it? [Shoot, what good are you?] It is only by putting our faith [gifts] into action, then and only then, does it transform into a vital life-saving entity. Training without action is null, zip, zilch.

Think about it.

Once you light off a round, what's the next thing you've got to do? Maneuver. A moving (working) target stays alive. If you maintain a fixed position, how long are you going to last?

Heb11:1 *Now faith is the substance of things anticipated, the evidence of things not [yet] seen.*

We've been training for this mission for quite a while. Our bodies and minds have been drilled. We operate as a finely tuned instrument. Our apostolic and prophetic leaders have laid out the mission based on His strategy. We can taste the combat environment. We see each player making his move in sync with the other team members. Just like Gideon, success is a given, we just need to carry it out. Because No matter what capabilities one possesses in munitions, weaponry, or electronics, it takes more than just having the ability. It takes more than just assembling the plan. It takes more than knowing that victory is assured. It takes action.

Faith requires putting action into the belief consideration. Faith is belief---during combat. It's putting the mental activity of our thoughts [things others cannot see] into physical action [for everyone to observe, make note of, and evaluate]. There's no other way to acquire faith, no operator work-arounds, and no suitable substitutes. Either you step out and do it, or you don't.

Inherent in taking any action is an element of risk. Apostles and Prophets take calculated risks every time they activate their gifts and whenever they provide direction and confirmation about His tasking. That's what makes them leaders. That's why the CINC continues to trust them with His vision and secrets. Like any human leader, they are not infallible. That's part of the risk. He wants us to move out and expand our territories and become mature in His gifts. This can only be accomplished by [seemingly] failure and success. It's the process of smelting the unwanted minerals and deposits out, prior to celebrating the arrival of the pure gold.

It's a well known fact, that when the war begins, all the paperwork and plans need to be modified because combat is an ever changing, dynamic action. We need to be prepared for the changes and variables we encounter during the engagement. Each mission can develop and reveal different variables. For example, shooting in San Antonio, TX in the Spring can be a real pleasure. Warm sun, no breeze, birds singing, bees buzzing, etc. But shooting in Minot, North Dakota during the same season, can be a challenge: frozen sky (sundogs), gale-force storms; winds whistling (not Dixie) through your parka; ears and nose [painfully] tingling, etc. Same mission; different variables. Funny how that works.

> Heb 11:6 *But without faith it is impossible to please Him;*

God is only as big as our faith in Him. Our faith is measured by God. It's doled out to us an increment at a time. As James said, we only have faith in what we're willing to do and act on. (James 2:17). So keep this in mind, He hasn't given us a spirit of fear. He wants us to go out in bold confidence, because He is with us.

Look at your life:
Who is the actor? Who is the audience?

God is the CINC, the JFC. He's maintaining SA for us; keeping aware of the big picture while we fight the righteous fight, in the combat zone. Toe-to-toe, building the foundation and revealing His plans and strategies to us. His warriors!

Chapter Forty One—

Amen

One final word before we go back out into the combat zone. This area is very important and cannot be taken lightly. Therefore, I'll go right to the pointy end of the spear. Grab a strap or buckle your harness, whichever is more appropriate.

The word Amen. What is it? What does it mean to you? What does it mean to your team? Your compadres. Is it something you say to wake yourself and others up from praying?

Amen comes from a root word meaning to build up or support; to foster as a parent or nurse; figuratively to become firm or faithful, to trust or believe, to be permanent; morally to be true or certain.

From this word comes its abstract meaning for faithfulness; truly. Amen, so be it, truth. "Do it, Lord." Amen needs to be said with confidence; enthusiasm; expectation. After you pray do you expect your requests have already been answered? Are you surprised by an answered prayer? Wow-ed? Or do you even notice when one is answered?

Wouldn't it be great? We've all seen the statue of the US Marines charging up the hill in Guadalcanal to plant the flag. On their way up to the top, what do you imagine they were saying? What did it sound like? Do you think they were leading a quiet processional for planting the flag in the ground? No, they were running, stumbling, grunting and, yelling at the top of their lungs, pushing each other to be the first to "top the hill". AMEN. Hallelujah! We reached the top. Mission accomplished. We're alive and the flag is flying.

Wouldn't it be great? Do you think they knew what was on the other side of the hill? Why didn't they wait to find out? Or did they put their trust in their leader?

In our prayers, after we request something, after we put our trust in Jesus, do we put our trust in Him and GO for it? Or do we sit around and wait for it to happen [and then are politely surprised it occurred]? Afterall, it could be something bad. There could be a field of jumping cactus just waiting to meet our acquaintance. You're absolutely right. There could be fields of cockleburs just waiting to attack your socks. You're certainly better off just chilling on your laurels. No doubt about it. More power to you. Afterall, you could get to the top of the hill, and the streets could be paved with gold. The Archangel Michael could be waiting to shake your hand, show you how to really wield the sword of the Lord, and demonstrate what a first class battle cry really sounds like. AMEN!

Remember, if you need to wake yourself or others up from prayer, use an alarm clock, a cowbell or even a hammer. Say, the prayer is over. But whatever you do, do NOT use Amen. Amen is a battle cry, a call for confident warfighters. Not to be confused with a weak-kneed plea for a wish [turn on the bubble machine Mr. Welk….a 1 and a 2, a wishing and a washing].

Amen. It's a verb. It invokes ACTION. Preserve it. Use "Amen" as a battle cry. Live your life for Jesus. Pray continuously.

AMEN. Do it Lord!

Chapter Forty Two—

Out Brief

You might not know Him, yet. You might not believe in Him, yet. But He knows your name, now. He took the ultimate sacrifice [the bullet] for you, then. Even before you were given a name.

That is what God did with His Son, Jesus. Jesus died for us in the battle with the world, our "self" and sin. He took the bullet for us.

Do you know the purpose or outcome of your life? Jesus knew His purpose was to save us by taking the bullet. Actually, "taking the bullet" trivializes the horror and agony of the death he suffered. His death was not a quick one. He knew prior to even coming to earth as a man, what the outcome was going to be. Thirty-three years of knowing the end result. If you knew the DTG (date-time-group) when you would be killed, how would it effect your life? Would you have a sense of urgency? A passion for all that you did?

Put yourself in His situation. God's Son sent to earth. A heavenly being put in human form to experience all the weaknesses, temptations, and joy (mental, physical, and emotional) of mankind. His life transformed into a construction worker. (Hod carriers, plumbers, masons, tile setters and carpenters have pride!) Some people believe Him. Others, especially those in governmental power, believe he posed a threat to [them] society and decided to kill him. Rather than just kill him quickly, or in a "humane" way, they decided to put him to the most shameful, humiliating, tortuous, public death possible....crucifixion.

Crucifixion, where the body is subjected to intense agony and numerous bouts of suffocation. Numerous bouts because just as the body is almost depleted from oxygen, the brain kicks into its emergency recovery mode, the muscles of the legs and torso are sent electrical charges to jerk in one more breath, thereby putting imminent death away for another couple minutes. This continues for hours upon end.

Jesus could have called for His Father to rescue Him. He could have called for angels to deliver Him from the torture. He could have Himself averted this situation. But He knew if this act wasn't accomplished, we (humans) would not have an alternative to death. I'm not only talking about physical death, when the body's machinery wears out and all the circuit breakers pop. I'm talking about eternal death. Death that is the base camp for the enemy. True. There's a lot of good people out there fighting against evil. But without Jesus, when the end-game finally arrives, the enemy, Satan, is going to be in control of them. No doubt about it. Without Jesus by your side, it's gonna happen.

His death is the key to our living. His blood literally washed away Satan's touch on our body. His resurrection, literally a death-defying act, is what unlocks the door to our eternal freedom from Satan's campsite. This is also what separates Jesus from the other [dead] human "greats". Mohammed, Buddha, Bob Marley, etc., were all great humans. However, they never did and never will push back the cloak of death. Jesus did.

Hey Satan, guess what? You lose; we win. Game over. Battle won! He blazed the pathway for warfighters to follow. He ensures survival for all, not just the fittest. The weak, the wounded, the trauma-suffering warfighters are all capable of not only surviving the war, but winning it. No losers. Just winners.

So, what's the requirement to win the battle with the world, self, and sin?

-The World can be defined as (1) following societal norms, (2) staying within the confines of the box, or (3) even living life on the edge. None of that matters.

There's only One requirement. Just One acknowledgement. One simple factor.

-Self can be described as good, bad, bright, dumb, ugly, or beautiful. None of that matters. Self is composed of body, soul, and spirit. Without Jesus, the spirit is empty. He is the only way to acquire the Spirit.

There's only One requirement. Just One acknowledgement. One simple factor.

-Sin is simply living without Jesus. Caring, sharing, good character, philanthropist, overall Mr. Niceguy. None of that conquers sin. You must reach out to Jesus.

There's only One requirement. Just One acknowledgement. One simple factor.

Believe in Him. That's it.

AMEN!

Chapter Forty Three—

Backword

We are warfighters! Warfighters, fighting for not only bodies and minds, but more importantly, for souls. We're <u>soul</u> warfighters, soul men. Yes, we are on a mission from God. Yes, you can attribute being a soul man to a much higher level than the Blues Brothers mission. Furthermore, if you decide to accept this mission, it will not be impossible. And no, there won't be a self-destructing tape involved when you've listened to the mission brief. Aye?

A warrior's credo:

Let me be known as a friend of Jesus.

A [mo' bettah] warrior's credo:

Let me be known as the enemy of Satan!

> *For everyone born of God conquers the world. 1John 5:4a*
>
> *They overcame him by the blood of the Lamb and by the word of their testimony!* Rev 12:11

This is the success story. *"We overcame..."*, that is WE defeated the enemy, the OPFOR.
WE are the victors over "...*him*"
CINCOPFOR, the devil, Satan.

> [Only] *by the blood of the Lamb* [Jesus] *and by the word of their testimony.*

"I believe & act."

Appendix A

Glossary and Acronyms

6: Six
> A positional reference based on the clock. Historically, "6" refers to the area behind that is hard to [tactically] defend.

Advanced Training
> Next layer after Basic Training. Shapes and hones specific skills. Preparation for choreographing combat.

AFSC: Air Force Specialty Code
> Describes assigned job tasks.

Alles klar: German for "all parts, facets, aspects, and technicalities are explicitly and completely understood."

ATO/ACO: Air Tasking Order/Air Control Order
> Who flies where, when, and how.

Basic Training
> Institutes critical foundational values: teamwork, physical and mental discipline.

BDU: Battle Dress Uniform
> Camouflaged fatigues.

BGD-6: Big Grey Desk with six drawers
> Standard government issue grey desk, rubber top. Pretty nasty looking. Formerly referred to as a BGD-5. Trust me, this is not a significant upgrade.

BLUFOR: True Blue Force
> The Good Guys.

BM: Battle Manager
> VIP seats managing the theater of operations.

BMC4I: Battle Management for Command, Control, Communications, Computers, and Intelligence
> Whew! That's a mouthful. If it's so intelligent why can't it be succinctly defined? Besides, what sane person would admit to being able to manage all this stuff?

C2: Command and Control
> Sideline battle management.

C4: C 1.. 2.. 3.. 4 [Boom!] ya.
> (Hey, I'm just guessing on this one.)
> Very powerful, compact plastic explosive. The choice of terrorists, saboteurs, and military explosive professionals.

Caps & Lims: Capabilities and Limitations
> What can be expected from a particular source.

CBO: Congressional Budget Office
> Holds the purse strings for funding and provides "rationale" for military spending. Affectionately referred to by the military as the Continuous Bludgeoning Offensive, Constant Beating Onslaught, etc.

CCD: Concealment, Camouflage, and Deception
> Hiding physical entities by any means available. Also applies to manipulating one's

perception to believe information that is not accurate.

Centralized Command
Provides priority tasking to shooters and information collectors.

CEP: Circular Error Probability
Information received and displayed within an ellipse. The ellipse has an assigned probability that the event actually occurred somewhere within its lines. The tighter the ellipse, the more useful or accurate the information.

CINC: Commander-in-Chief
Numero Uno. Can't get any higher than this person.

CONOP: Concept of Operations
A declarative document offering a description for functional employment of specific equipment, required personnel, support, etc.

CSAR: Combat Search and Rescue
Extremely high-risk mission. Many crew members committed to risking their lives in order to retrieve one Good Guy from Bad Guy land. Only teamwork can make this successfully happen.

CTP: Common Tactical Picture
> A clear display for the battle manager depicting all the information (air, space, ground, surface, and subsurface) he wants and needs to maximize his decision-making capabilities. Note: this "big picture" does not yet exist [on earth].

Data: Computers exchanging binary information between each other.

Decentralized Execution
> Shooter/information collector determines specific procedure for servicing the target.

D.I./T.I.: Drill Instructor/Training Instructor
> Initially, your own personal living nightmare. Afterwards, one who prepared you to successfully engage the enemy in combat.

DOD: Department of Defense
> In simplified terms, this refers to the military.

Einbahnstraße: This is from the German language. It is not a street dedicated to a famous person, but rather denotes a "1-way street."

EMI: Electromagnetic Interference
> Has another transmitter ever temporarily blocked your communication when you're on the CB? That's an extremely simple, but real representation of EMI.

EMP: Electromagnetic Pulse
> Usually associated with the environment immediately after a nuclear explosion. Electronic equipment not able to resist this

huge surge in electrical power (cars, computers, telephone networks, etc.) will be inoperative [forever].

Fratricide
> Killing one of our own. Can occur frequently because of misidentification.

HF: High Frequency (radio)
> Ah, the luxuries of static piercing radio; voices talking out from a hollow tunnel.

ID: Identification
> Part of the "Sort 'em and Shoot 'em" process.

Intel: Intelligence
> Pretty much an oxymoron when referring to the military or government in general. However, in this case it's only a shortened version of the word.

IPB: Intelligent Preparation for the Battlefield
> This is used in lieu of the military's Intelligence Preparation of the Battlefield. Think about the great difference between these two. The military's definition is only the foundation for the Christian Warfighter IPB.

JFC: Joint Forces Commander
> The person who has the "stick". Numero Uno. The head honcho for this theater of operations.

JMTOP: Joint Multi-Tactical Digital Information Link Operating Procedures
> Governs a very complex operational environment by stipulating how a sensor can provide inputs.

Joint Environment
> Different players, perceptions, and routines requiring synchronized action. Not an easy task. Involving one or more of the sister services: Army, Navy, Air Force, or Marine Corps.

LIMFAC: Limiting Factors
> Don't expect too much; here's all we can provide.

MOS: Military Occupation Specialty
> Describes assigned job tasks.

NCTR: Non-Cooperative Target Recognition
> A means to identify hostile targets.

OPFOR: Opposing Force
> The Bad Guys.

OPTASKLINK
> Otherwise known as the Communications Plan.

PC: Politically Correct
> A man-made rationale for doing wrong, acceptably.

PsyOps: Psychological Operations
> Mind games. Success and defeat are most often determined from the mental picture.

RFW: Request for Wisdom
A play on words for Request for Information (RFI).

ROE: Rules of Engagement
Laws of combat governing the operational environment.

SA: Situational Awareness
Knowing all pertinent aspects regarding the current operational environment.

Sabotage/Espionage
Nothing put pure, outright skullduggery.

SCIF: Sensitive Compartmented Information Facility
A Super "Secret Squirrel" area.

SEABEES:
Armed, heavy equipment operators. The Navy trains these guys exceptionally well to get the construction phase going usually in [pretty darn] hostile territory.

Sensor[s]:
Ultimately, a piece of equipment that uses different sources of information to differentiate between good guys and bad guys.

SIAP: Single Integrated Air Picture
All airborne [and many ground/surface] entities are identified, accounted for, and individually represented to all participants

and observers. This too does not yet exist [on earth].

Sin
: An acronym for Stinkin' Satan Is Near.

Snake Eaters
: Special Operations people that are usually the first one's into an area. These guys won't be available for CNN to film them.

Spin Doctor
: An acronym for Stinkin' Satan's Prototype Is Near.

SPINS: Special Instructions
: Significant "don't forget" information.

SPIT: Stinkin' Phony Intellect and Tongue
: Only "loyal" enough to offer lip service.

TI: Training Instructor
: See DI/TI.

TOE: Table of Equipment
: List detailing required (mandatory) equipment for a given system or mission.

TTP: Tactics, Techniques, and Procedures
: The choreography of combat.

UHF: Ultra High Frequency (radio)
: Chatter and clatter on the radio.

VHF: Very High Frequency (radio)
: More chatter and clatter via radio.

The Warfighter's Guide Order Form

Use this convenient order form to order additional copies of
The Warfighter's Guide

Please Print:

Name_____

Address_____

City_____ **State**_____

Zip_____

Phone(   )_____

_____ copies of book @ $10.00 each $ _____
Postage and handling @ $1.00 per book $ _____
FL residents add 6 % tax $ _____
Total amount enclosed $ _____

Make checks payable to RnBCo.

**Send to Richard Conant
34 Indian Bayou Drive • Destin, FL 32541**